My Heart And My Mind

My Heart And My Mind

◆

An American Muslim Patriot Speaks

By Bajram Angelo Koljenovic
With James Nathan Post

iUniverse, Inc.
New York Lincoln Shanghai

My Heart And My Mind
An American Muslim Patriot Speaks

iUniverse, Inc.

For information address:
iUniverse, Inc.
2021 Pine Lake Road, Suite 100
Lincoln, NE 68512
www.iuniverse.com

ISBN: 0-595-31282-9

Printed in the United States of America

Contents

NOTE xi

AN HISTORICAL PERSPECTIVE. 8

ABOUT THE RELIGION 20

ABOUT A BIRTHDAY PARTY 25

IT'S NOT EASY BEING JEWISH EITHER. 31

IT'S NOT ALL IN THE MIDDLE EAST. 42

STILL A BOSNIAN, AMERICAN?. 49

AMBASSADOR ANGELO 58

A PEACE CONFERENCE 67

AGENT ANGELO. 72

THE ISLAMIC BOMB 85

THE CRUELEST BLOW 91

A CALL TO RIGHTEOUSNESS 95

ABOUT THE AUTHORS. 99

Acknowledgements

I would first like to acknowledge, in the far background, my good friend Lorie, who has typed endlessly and tirelessly, and has made it possible to put this book into cover sooner than I thought possible. She is the best listener I have ever worked with. James Nathan Post, co-author of our epic historical novel <u>Blood of Montenegro</u>, once again contributed his wordmanship and unique viewpoint. His contribution in work and talent, and in drawing forth my most intimate feelings guided me into finishing that wonderful semi-biographical story, and into writing this very personal book to follow it. I hope will reach readers with excitement and pleasure beyond my belief for the success of my personal story. His friendship is much appreciated and honored in my heart and my family. I also wish to express my respect and affection for Braho Mrkuljic, an honorable man of the highest character who has been both supporter and inspiration to me through many of the hard times in my life.

This book is dedicated to all of the armed forces of the United States of America, our military forces who protect this great nation from harm's way and who have given me, and all of us, a chance for a free and joyful life. I am honored that you have recognized me as your fellow citizen, and that you place your own lives at risk in order for me to enjoy the many benefits of that citizenship. May God give you wisdom, and guide you to a long, prosperous, and healthy life. May God bless every one of you who have worn and are wearing the uniform of this great nation.

Special thanks:

To my parents,

My mother Nurija,

My father, Halim,

Thank you for giving me life, and teaching me right from wrong;

To my wife, Man Kiu,

And our children,

My son, Neli,

My daughter, Nadira

And my littlest one, six year old Halim Shaoyang, whom I must regularly take to the recruiting office of our armed forces for visits, at his insistence.

Thank you all for making it possible for my dreams to come true.

Bajram Angelo Koljenovic

NOTE

My participation in this book is a bit difficult for me to define, more than an editor, but hardly a true co-author. This book is a very personal statement, and I have tried as much as possible to help my literary collaborator clearly identify his viewpoint, and to express his feelings, without interjecting more of my own than hopefully will make for good reading. My respected friend Angelo is an honest and passionate man, a man who has proved his patriotism in word and in action, and who deserves the best opportunity to present himself in this way. I am honored to have had this opportunity to help him present his heart and his mind to the people of America and to the world.

James Nathan Post

I was not born an American. I chose to be an American, and I chose to leave behind the land of my youth and the land of my family when I came to America. Citizenship was not my birthright, and I had to work and study in order to earn it. For me it was a privilege and an accomplishment to become an American citizen. I became a patriot out of my learning and my experience, and my conviction that the principles and ideals which define America are the pinnacle of all mankind's social progress. For me to call myself an American patriot is a great honor, and I feel humble to be able to offer my loyalty, my support, my admiration, and my life to this fine land, to this wonderful people. It is my greatest pride and honor to be able to say, "These are my countrymen, and this is my homeland."

I was born and raised a Muslim. Until I was a young adult, my experience with other religion consisted of watching from a distance the village celebrations and conflicts of the Roman Catholic and Orthodox churches, both of whom at times looked down on us Muslims, and from a greater distance the Jewish, who were even more a minority than we. It was only later, after much reading and meeting other people that I learned enough about those religious forms and about the God they describe to embrace my family's form of Islam by choice. The God I have discovered all those religions to be seeking, and the desire for peace, community, and respect for all His children they each call for are the most true and most important things in the world. If people actually lived as though they believed in those things, we could have Heaven on earth.

Having such common ideals and such common faith, one might think they should quickly come to an agreement, and would welcome each other in brotherhood and celebration. Having such love for my country, and for my God, one might think I should feel close in the embrace of my community and welcomed by the smiling faces of my people, my American countrymen, my brothers and sisters. How sad it is that instead the world is in chaos fighting over those religious distinctions, and in America I find myself increasingly isolated, as Muslims are being identified and demonized as an unwelcome minority, a threat to real Americans. How could such fine ideals, such devout faith, and such patriotic devotion produce such terrible results?

It is easy to point to the implacable momentum of history, from the Diaspora to the fall of Rome, the beginning of Islam, the Ottoman Empire, the rise and

1

division of Catholicism, to the newborn nation of Israel. It is easy to point to those precepts in the doctrines of each of their religions which led to the nit-picking exclusivity over which the several sects continue to fight. It is easy enough to see what has been going on these five millennia, and how the history has been driven by the precepts of these interwoven religions, as they quarrel about probate rights to the promises they believe God made to their and our common ancestor Abraham. Even so saying, I don't presume to explain it, much less to be able to offer some clever insight that might help the world to correct it, whatever that might mean. I hope at best to show how one person can try to do some good in response to the madness and turbulence, the violence that no one in the world's leadership seems to have the conviction or the will to assert the power to avert, a one way trip to hell.

We are perhaps born equal in the eyes of God, but we each have unique heritage, as though each of us is born with a hand of cards. That is part of our fate, and whatever we do with it that does not change. It was my fate for better or for worse that I was born to a Muslim family in a little village high in the mountains of a country that was then called Yugoslavia. I was born in Montenegro, one of the eight once independent states which made up the tapestry of Yugoslavia. As a Minority, I am ethnically a Bosnian from the province of Sandjak, and Montenegro. To the north and west of us, in Bosnia and Herzegovina, Muslims are the majority, but it was my fate that in Montenegro we were a minority. It was many years before I began to understand the stories told about my father's generation, and his father's, and how we had been persecuted and murdered by our neighbors the Orthodox Serbs, Roman Catholic Croats, Albanians, and Italians.

Today, as it has been for hundreds of years, life in that Balkan region is troubled and violent. Some of my family still lives in that same village, and others have become American citizens as I have. We are separated, but not apart. Though I am an American, are they not still my family when the troops come marching up the streets? Worse, when my American government and the rest of the so called democratic world stands aside and watches the troops come marching to round up my ancestral people, are they not then still my family? When a few non-faithful Muslims whose beliefs lead them to depart from the peace of Islam conduct acts which make Americans misunderstand, fear, and hate all they identify with Islam, must I then not try to help my family for fear of appearing to support those who oppose America? Is it possible in the complicated world of today to be a Muslim patriot in the United States of America? I intend to prove that it certainly is. There are millions of people of my faith who are devoted to and love and are staunch supporters of the state of the union and stars and stripes. There are certainly some who do not share our American way of life.

I wish I could just put the real names of everybody involved in this book. I would like to be able to drag the villains out into the light, and let everybody know just what they did, and for whom. Much as possible, I'll do that. One character I would like to identify unfortunately has the same name as a certain beloved celebrity, who doesn't deserve the misunderstanding that would naturally take place, so I'll just keep him on a first-name basis. I would also like to be able to bring out the heroes, and to let some good people take well-deserved applause for doing jobs that must forever be kept secret. Sadly, as crypto people, they get crypto names, and no curtain calls. What I have not done is to create composite or fictional characters to fill out the drama in an otherwise historical scene. My opinions and my conclusions are based upon my on experience, and my own limited knowledge of history that I am very comfortable with, and they are entirely my own, but the people in this book are all real. Some names have been changed to protect the privacy of the innocent.

My mother's father Ebrahim Vukelj was a young Ottoman officer when the empire fell in 1912. When he was captured while saving the life of Vojvoda Borichic, one of the officers of the victorious King Nicola of Montenegro, my Grandpa became a friend and favorite of the King, who was an Orthodox Catholic. Sometimes jokingly referred to as "Nicola's little Turk," my grandfather was able to remain one of the local aristocracy, and he had a fine farm from which he fed the armies of a succession of leaders and invaders who came through the passes surrounding the little valley where our village of Gusinje sits surrounded by the most beautiful mountains and rivers. At times because of the political feuds and wars the banks and the river have been covered with innocent blood, but even then the river looks so calm and peaceful if one can see the nature and beauty. In the calm flowing of the river one can for sure hear the voices and cries of the innocent souls the river has carried through the centuries at times all the way to the Black Sea. I wonder if the beautiful lush valley and the Trojan mountains will ever see the peace, which seems like even God himself has forgotten. For whatever reason, men have chosen to solve their differences with the sword and barrel of the gun. I have finally realized if we give ourselves a chance and an honest thought to communicate with honesty we wouldn't have a need to kill each other. Children would no longer be butchered, raped and thrown on wooden sticks, instead they would be playing and enjoying their parents at their farms to provide a home, which every child and human deserves with dignity.

Many years later my Grandpa would pay back the favors he had enjoyed by hiding the King in his own home while he was being pursued by the conquering Mussolini who just a few years earlier had invaded Ethiopia with his mighty fascist army which had no regards for the human life. Even then, the King of Ethiopia asked the United Nations for help to save his people from the butchery of the fascist army. They didn't lift a finger. It looks to me as if some members of the UN did not understand the consequences that would follow, just as it happened. Mussolini's ambition was to bring back Roman glory. Ten years later the only glory he received was by being left hanging upside down by his own people for betraying the loyalty of the people who entrusted the power to him which he got by overthrowing the King and Queen.

My grandfather was not pleased when his daughter chose to marry my father Halim Koljenovic. It was not that he did not like and respect the serious young man, but he knew that like one of his own sons, Halim was a Communist. He had managed to endure the fall of the Ottoman well enough, and more than one war since, but the idea of the idealistic authoritarian labor-union collectivism of Communism actually becoming the law of the land was not something he welcomed.

Ebrahim knew Halim had carried the burden of being the man of his family a long time, as his father Bajram Koljenovic while still young had died of malaria, a disease for which there was no cure then, in battle in the lush swamps of Bojana river in Albania. It was a serious blow to the family, as Bajram had been a strong leader and local hero first cousin of the great Ottoman officer and hero, Jafer Pasha Koljenovic, Governor of today's country on the shores of the Indian Ocean called Yemen. Jafer Pasha was decorated and ordained with a provincial coat of arms in his honor, as Governor of Yemen and the Arabian Peninsula. Turkey has also named their military academy in his honor. My grandfather Bajram was already the "Godfather" of our kolektiv Zadruga, our organized extended family. This ancient family based social structure has long been the fundamental way of keeping order and justice in our culture. Always more powerful in the people's lives than the government, it is the real thing behind the stereotype which makes up the popular image of the mafia. It is about family duty, and about blood. Bajram, my Grandpa, was the man, the patriarch, his young age notwithstanding, and when his judgments were crossed, blood flowed. You can walk today right to the corner in Gusinje where he personally shot a man dead on Friday morning and then pulled a handkerchief out of his sash, wiped his revolver and then threw the white handkerchief on the man he had just killed, while everyone in town watched, all dressed up to shop and socialize. He was the man, and then he was gone, and it was all left to my father, Halim and his brother Halit.

Halim was one of the best-educated young men in town, one who excelled in several local offices, and eventually became the Chief of Police. Like Ebrahim his father in law, he was good enough at his job that he kept it under a succession of changes of government. Though he was very influential in bringing to power his comrade Josip Broz Tito, he later fell out of favor with the party, taken as a threat intellectually who was capable of growing in the ranks of the Communist party. No wonder some members that he himself had installed in positions have burned the rug under his feet and accused him of favoring Stalinism over Titoism. That cost him five years on the rock island prison called Goli Otok, the Naked Island, at the north Adriatic Ocean where blistering cold winds are known to exceed sixty miles per hour. One may expect weather like that in winter at times for three of four months at a time. The summers are hot and almost unbearable, and you could fry an egg on any exposed metal surface at any given time of day. One cannot imagine being imprisoned in such a place with no place to hide from the sun nor the blistering cold in winter. If I were looking for a place to show you hell on earth there would be no need to travel any farther than Naked Island. There is where my father had paid a price and his faith had been decided. Among my earliest memories is watching him being dragged from his bed by armed men, officers of the same party he had devoted his life to creating, soldiers of the same local bureaucracy and militia that he himself had organized and run.

While he was away in prison, and when he came home to take a menial job, I grew up watching the insensitive and implacable machinery of the Communist state being manipulated by the greedy and the vindictive so as to gradually strip away all that we had, reducing us from a strong self-supporting family to a subsistence client of the state. All that was good and right and healthy about the life we had lived was destroyed. When my mother died while being shuffled through the endless and expensive process of seeking and suffering the communist state's "free" medical treatment—which apparently did not apply for my mother because of the political persecution of my father—I resolved that I would free myself of that life one day. I promised myself I would find a place where the job of the government was to help people create good lives for themselves, and then to let them live those lives, a place where it didn't matter if you were a Muslim or a Jew, or a monkey worshipper, you weren't going to get rounded up and shot for it.

It didn't take me long to find such a place. As a young soldier in the Army of Yugoslavia, I was trained as a commando, and then after being wounded, I served in a staff office of Topcider in Belgrade working among Tito's favorite generals, including Ljubichic General Isidor Papa, where I got a quick education in the realities of world politics. After my tour of duty in the military I went to live in Italy and took a job and discovered the vast world of trade and power which lies along or beyond such boundaries as governments and laws, respecting none. Though I saw quite a bit of the world, and I had friends and family in many places, it was clear to me that only one place offered me the potential, the opportunity, and the freedom to fulfill my dreams, and that place was the United States of America.

I was right.

I boarded a Pan Am jet at Lido di Ostia, on the outskirts of Rome at Fiumicino Airport, set in beautiful lush meadows near the banks of the Tiber River. My first grand American experience was eight hours later after landing in New York City at Kennedy airport, a quick tour by my friend in a brand new 1971 Le Mans Pontiac to see Grand Concourse Avenue and of course Yankee Stadium and New York national monuments as well as forty second street and Broadway. With the thrill that I had already, what I saw there was a little man with deformed feet, heels in the front and toes in the back. I drifted for the moment in my soul and my heart to my father's home in Montenegro. My elderly Grandmother used to tell me stories of such a little man with deformed feet, who was made to dance in circles by demons. Even with all the people around me and all the pleasure I was having at that moment I found myself alone and my heart was beating in my chest. I wanted to be back in that wonderful old kitchen room, next to that wooden stove and my sweet Grandmother drinking Turkish coffee with her. I realized that was not possible. I have chosen a new life on my own. There in New York I saw just such a little man, a simple man with a little problem of deformity, and he looked so happy and cheerful I wanted to know his name. I introduced myself and I couldn't help looking at his feet. Without hesitation, in a very polite language he asked me not to worry or be sorry, he is just fine the way he is and told me that his ancestors are from Italy, although he does not speak the language. "Please permit me to call you my giant little friend," I said, "big in heart and small in body. You have just brightened my day, beyond my expectations."

He told me his name was Julio and he lived in Forest Hills, just across the park near Yellowstone and Queens Boulevard, and he invited me to come and say hello at the Italian Restaurant, Tutto Bene. He told me not to worry, as to know New York is to know America. I didn't fully understand at that moment what he was trying to tell me, but I eventually understood he meant I should immerse myself in the life of New York, to learn to think quick, to think American, and to set my sights high. So I set myself to fulfill the promise of the phrase I heard them say, "Go West, young man." I soon found the open space and opportunity of the new frontier, and I knew I had been right for dreaming about America.

AN HISTORICAL
PERSPECTIVE

In ancient times there was a road which led from the city of Babylon (which means "gate to the god") to the mouth of the Black Sea in the Mediterranean, and then across to the valley of the Danube River. It is the consensus of paleo-anthropologists that pre-historic man evolved into record keeping man among these beautiful and ancient wonderlands called Babylon, Persia, Phoenicia, and Assyria and the beautiful fertile valley of Anatolia. The Rivers which travel from the edge of the Black Sea to the mouth of the Persian Gulf, the Euphrates and Tigris, were said in ancient times to be the source of the life of the Garden of Eden. The rich plain between them became known as the Fertile Crescent. Whether or not it was the birthplace of mankind, this rich plain certainly deserves to be called its cradle of civilization. The Semitic peoples, both the Arabs and the Hebrews, the Aryans, the Indians and Vedic people, all have been shown to have bloodlines that came from there long before the beginnings of recorded history. It was there that mankind first began to use the magic of written symbol, and to use that magic to conduct organized trade, to record stories of the past, and to describe a desired future, beginning the functions of accounting, history, and prophecy.

If I wanted to thank anyone among my ancient forefathers for bringing about the present day reality I enjoy, I might choose King Cyrus the Great. His victory over Babylonia already profoundly affected the course of history, but things would have been very different if he had been one of the many conquerors who burned and looted and killed the people he conquered. Instead he chose to be merciful to his new subjects, and to give them freedoms they had never known, and rewarded them with citizenship in his empire. His citizens were free to move anywhere within his empire, and from 535 to 530 BC he let more than fifty thousand Palestinians of the then new Jewish faith (there was no Christianity or Islam then) return to their claimed ancient homeland on the Jordan River. That single act made it possible for the later formation of all the religions that we still meditate on, and still use as justification for brutally killing each other.

Without his open-mindedness, I doubt that the story of Abraham would even be remembered, and the Virgin Mary would never have given birth to the Christ. There would be no Romans and Rabbis crucifying the men they felt had threatened them and their position. There would be no Islam either. Considering all of the profound events that have happened since his reign it is no wonder they call him Cyrus the Great. As I write this, I feel as though his hand is on my shoulder, and he is assuring me. I can almost hear his whisper in a gentle voice and the weight of his hand gently on my shoulder as he was saying to me, "Angelo, my child, don't worry, I knew what I was doing, after all, you are all my children and I am proud of you and your successes." I wish I could put my hand on his and tell him that our success towards each other as humans and Man has not been that good.

We have since found new religions, new gods, new prophets, and we have divided each other, not in ethnic or cultural differences but religious differences which we call Christianity and Islam. A child was born, in a land in Gaza on the west bank which you yourself, Cyrus the Great, sent the people for refuge or economical reasons long after you were marching through the ancient lands and the lush and beautiful valleys surrounding the Black Sea. Turbulence that has come after the triumph of your successes has revolutionized the ancient world. With all the good and evil deeds that have transpired through the ages new empires and rulers have been born. Unfortunately not with the hand of giving and mercy but with oppression and killing and flowing rivers of blood.

A child was born there we call now the Christ, who was supposed to be sent to save mankind from their own damnation by paying with his own life on the cross for the sins of the world from your time to ours for eternity. We have used the name of Christ in fighting many wars, and used religion to make war against each other and every time we raise the sword to strike or take someone's life we have used the name of Christ or of Muhammad as an excuse to damn ourselves with such destruction that we even experience now in our century, and all in the name of God. Through the centuries all the religions have practiced forceful acceptance of their faiths or risk alienation and it has happened in the last five hundred years in our new found land America.

Extermination of most all of the native South American people, Inca, Aztec and many others has been done in the name of God. From the North Pole, the Bering Sea to the South Pole, Terra del Fuego, extermination has occurred. By way of colonization, and introduction of an old religion into a new land, preachers and Conquistadores swept the land, converting the natives and subjecting them, and eventually placing them in conflict with each other. All over the world, in Yugoslavia, Rwanda, and dozens of other places, people have tried to exterminate each other because one group believes Christ is God and the other believes he was just a prophet and a messenger of God. Jewish Rabbis have said Christ should not come as a carpenter or a fisherman but in much greater power. Perhaps they were expecting someone like a Greek Zeus, or a divine conqueror, but for myself, even though I am not of the Christian faith, I think his mission was simply that of an honest but poor man preaching a better life for humankind.

How easily people forget the contributions that the people of the Middle East and Islam have made to the progress of man. Two thousand years of prosperity of the great civilizations from the Persians to the Moors, before Alexander through the Pharaohs, Constantine, and the Ottomans, produced advances in architecture, science, astronomy, mathematics, medicine, linguistics, and literature. From to Granada and Cordoba, to Malaga, our Middle Eastern ancient Persian forefathers have left us the most and beautiful places as gifts to enjoy, the most profound beauty built by men of the Middle East of Islamic faith in Spain, Tunisia in Libya, Casablanca in Morocco, to Jerusalem and the Petra in Jordan valley, to the garden of Eden in the land of Babylon, to Mecca and Medina in the high desert of Saudi Arabia.

When Europe was living in the dark ages as small tribal communities, the Middle East was a land of milk and honey, with trade all over the known world, and with scientific accomplishments not matched for hundreds of years in the West. When the Catholic monasteries given credit for the "discoveries" of the Renaissance were boasting libraries of twenty or thirty books of hand lettered parchment, the Islamic library of Cordoba, in Spain, had almost half a million bound books in Arabic written on fine paper made from the same hemp whose resin was used as a medicinal analgesic. Many of the great Greek texts translated into Latin and kept in the monasteries were translated from Arabic translations of the long lost Greek texts. One of these describes a series of experiments at the Islamic university at Cordoba involving the construction of feathered wing-like devices intended for human flight, pre-dating Da Vinci by almost five hundred years. They had highly developed studies of astronomy and navigation, and had accurately calculated the diameter of the earth hundreds of years before Columbus sailed. Using numerals taken from mathematical script in India, they developed the modern form of number notation based on place designation and the use of the zero that made mathematics possible. They created spherical trigonometry and algebra, an Arabic word meaning "bone-setting" which was used to describe its inventor's method for solving quadratic equations. Lack of this system of mathematics was a major limitation to the Romans' ability to progress in science.

It is one of the basic precepts of the Koran, for better or for worse, that in God's time, all of the world shall be united in Islam, and all of its people shall live in accordance with its wisdom, by will and by law. So it has always seemed quite natural and appropriate to the leaders of Islam that bringing more and more of the world into the tent of Islam should be something vigorously and religiously pursued, by profiling the religion in a way that masses would accept it without use of force or perhaps sometimes by conquest. It has been proposed in the history of Islam that the Great Wall of China was not built to stop invaders from inside China, although we have had many different opinions. Through the history scholars and historians have debated it, many believe the Great Wall of China was built to stop the spread of Islam. It didn't really work, as the Islamic religion has grown inside of China more to more than a hundred and seventy million people.

To my astonishment almost after fourteen hundred years even in China the religion of Islam still has not been understood as religion of compassion and mercy and giving. Instead sadly with the help of the Western world (and I am one of the Westerners who at times even as a Muslim misunderstand my own religion) it is seen as a violent and predatory force in the world. This is not because of the fault of Koran but because of greed and misrepresentation of the Imams who have been blinded by greed for power and who have created local's customs and traditions having nothing to do with Koran and religion. Separation of church and state is the only way that two institutions can correctly coexist, never be integrated as one. The Law of the Land is guidance for peace and safety and the well being for the citizens. The Koran and the Bible are in my opinion scriptures for meditation after a hard day of work. In my personal experience I have found it useful to meditate and to thank God or Allah, which mean the same, perhaps for his guidance and health for me and my family and my country. It has always brought me inner peace and forgiveness for whatever that may be in my soul. Going back to recorded history of the creation of Islam in Mecca and Medina, in a period of only the fourteen hundred years after the proclaiming of Islam by the prophet Mohammed, the Arab people all quit fighting among themselves and united to bring Islam to the world as the Koran instructs them to do, and promises them it will. The result was an empire even greater than that of Rome.

During the five hundred thirty years of the Ottoman reign, there was relative peace in the Middle East. Then in the late nineteenth century, many Middle East countries allied with Western Europe to liberate themselves from the Turks. They believed the promises of the West that they would not intervene in their internal affairs to occupy them, but only to liberate them, and then to trade with them. The result was the liberation of the trans-continental Jordan peninsula by British and allied forces. They were not called unbelievers and infidels then, but liberators. The allies were waging a major war with the Turks to liberate the Middle East and Egypt, the whole of the North African continent, the Persian Gulf states, the lands of Babylon and Assyria, the high desert of Arabia, Mecca and Medina, home of the prophet Mohammed, and the birthplace of Abraham, Babylon, today's modern Iraq, and land of the Byzantine Empire, Ethiopia, and the Somali Peninsula.

What was advertised as a humanitarian political agenda was of course an economic and strategic agenda without letting the Arabs know what was under their beds, that which we in the West call "Black Gold" and the native Americans called poisoned water. The Industrial Revolution had come to the West, and the Westerners had realized that the domination of the Middle East's mineral rich oil fields must be accomplished at any cost, political or military. It became clear that Arabia was the gateway to winning the Industrial Revolution, as the black gold deposits in the oil fields of the Arabian peninsula and the rest of the Middle East are far greater than the fields of Texas and Oklahoma, wealth of a scale never before dreamed of. It became of the greatest importance to the West to have control of that resource.

To do so, you must conquer by military strength and create internal political weakness to control the masses. The western allies whether by extraordinary luck or by understanding tribal culture brought them together with the promise of liberation from the Ottoman empire which had dominated their lives five hundred years. The latest ruler of Arabian Peninsula in the late 1800's and beginning of the 1900's was no one else but Jafer Pasha Koljenovic, my ancestor. They called him an iron fist, a reputation well earned, not as an oppressor, but with a firm rule of law. He became highly respected as who knew that you do not back off from your beliefs in the strength of the internal character of the individual and of the culture. By the might of his military, in each rebellion during the Ottoman rule rebels always found themselves the losers. As it was well known that various tribes sought to break up the empire or to destroy the peace, the western world made its overtures to them. Their promise to liberate the middle East from Ottoman rule was received with enthusiasm. Nobody knew how to read between the lines. When England said to them, "Your liberation has waited too long," it wasn't liberation of the Arabs they were talking about. It was in fact a second crusade, to pay back King Saladin for kicking out King Richard from Jerusalem, the birthplace of Christ the peacemaker, and sending Richard home with a doubly broken heart. He had been allowed to visit the holy place, and he had lost his princess to Saladin's charms and good looks.

The Kingdom of Great Britain had her thoughts set right, realizing that they didn't have to proclaim themselves to be crusading for Christianity. This was the chance for the Christian world to walk through Mecca and the Muslim world without being shot at. What a way to dominate. Turkey got smart, and her generals pulled back to the original national borders under the command of Kemal Ataturk. Young and western educated, he defeated allied forces on the banks of Dardanelles and Istanbul. It was not just a defeat, it was such a blow out that even the name of the city of Constantinople was changed to Istanbul. Turkey had survived again.

England and France and the rest of the allies got only one wish, Jerusalem. I can hardly disagree with the triumph that was achieved after the tragic failure of Phillip Augustus of France and King Richard's crusader army, which had committed the most atrocities in the history of any army. Phillip was lucky to go back to France after losing most of his army fighting many losing battles. They were granted permission by Saladin to go back home with some surviving crusaders. By the time they got to Austria, Richard was arrested by the Duke of Austria who had enough reason to try him for failing the Holy Roman Empire and not capturing Jerusalem and the holy land. Augustus of France was lucky. Augustus of France was permitted to go to France and rule his country. Richard was not permitted to go to England, instead was arrested by the Duke of Austria in the name of the Roman Empire and imprisoned for two years. After his release he was granted permission to go back to England, which he did for a very short period of time.

When Richard first left England on his crusade with the rest of the European nobles and Kings, he thought in his mind that England was invincible and prosperous. Upon his return he became disappointed and unfortunately he found that England was nothing of what he thought it was. By traveling thousands of miles through then Anatolia, today's Turkey, and northern Syria and the coast of Lebanon, he must of got a taste of the culture, strong traditions, awesome architecture, advanced bath houses, and libraries with millions of books and literature in Greek, Latin, Arabic and Hebrew. In England nothing like that yet existed before or in his time. He must have seen his country after all this experience as poor and backward and practically in the dark ages. I assume he must have thought that the task of responsibility would be enormous for him to try to modernize and bring England to the level of Syria or Austria, or perhaps Rome. He must have felt heartbroken by not being able to snap his finger and make England stand up next to the rest of the nations, proud and tall.

I think he then decided to leave and went back to France on a suicide mission, which is exactly what he got I think, looking for a honorable death. History has portrayed him, that is, England's history, as a noble patriot and hero. I think there is enough room there for an intellectual argument or discussion for the historians to argue his successes and failures. If I would scale them from one to ten, I would characterize him as a wonderful man, a most fascinating dreamer for whom not a single dream he had came true in his lifetime. With no doubt, the dreams that Richard had, after all have come true through the generations of his royal bloodline. From the time of his unfortunate death in France, England has prospered and grown beyond even King Richard's dreams as a nation and would fulfill all the dreams that he never got to see.

I think he would approve of today's England, a proud nation, to be respected. They had even fulfilled his dream of capturing Jerusalem, and creating a new state of Israel. This was an unimaginable victory one can only dream about, though nobody dared to brag about it or wave the flag of Christianity. The holy land was retaken and England got most of North Africa, sharing the rest with other European countries. England got the biggest and best piece of the pie from the shores of Indian and Atlantic Oceans. The growth of the UK empire was astonishingly cleaver and timely fast. It seemed England had developed communication to give the colonies local control of their civil daily ways of life without interrupting cultures and traditions. In that way they won the hearts and minds of the majority of their colonies, from India to Africa and North America to Australia.

The French on the other hand, with their Napoleonic complex of ignorance, failed to win the hearts and minds of any of their conquered new colonies. How could they after all? The army they had then and today consist of the lowest of the low life from every culture and religion, from the homeless and unfortunate, illegitimate born, criminals, and thrill killers. They have given them the well-deserved name French Legionnaires. I have a suggestion for the French people today. It would be best if they would dismantle such an organization. They are killers and rapists and murderers, and they have blood on their hands up to their shoulders with the blessing of the French government, and their little Napoleon, their national hero and respected leader, Charles De Gaulle. He wanted to make Algeria a new republic of France. For whatever reason other French politicians and many people didn't approve, but before they left Africa, they left a trail of blood and destruction. That hardly fits a prescription of medicine to help the sick nation of Algeria to be well. Instead the French prescription was a hand full of poison, and bullets from their guns. Hundreds of thousands of innocent people were murdered throughout Algeria the other French colonies.

In many stories of real battles it has been told that French murderers and irresponsible forces gunned down hundreds or perhaps thousands of North African horse riders. It is a good example of how they felt about the people who were the war victims, whom they portrayed as uncivilized or uncultivated. The French and European noticed cultural differences between themselves and North African people. They saw people from the Barbary States as barbarians. They dare not to tell the truth to themselves.

Unfortunately somehow all of us are in our own little world. It could be a little room or a little garden in the back of your house, or a royal palace home, but it is still a little place away from the reality of the rest of the world. The Queen of Spain, who gave the Italian adventurer Columbus all the money he wanted to go look for the new world, was not happy with what she had at home, so the story goes. As Columbus was trying to find India, the Queen was getting rid of certain undesirable subjects among her citizens. She decided that anybody who did not accept Roman Christianity must leave Spain or die. After all, Spain was newly a Christian country. Conversion from Islam to Christianity happened after the Moors left Spain. With mass exodus of her undesirable citizens, she was left with a pot of gold of businesses and real estate that could not be carried out of the country.

Currency was in gold coins at the time, was not allowed to be taken out of the country by the people exiting it. The strategy had worked with enormous gains for the rest of the citizens. After all, the exodus numbered in millions. The wealth that was left was given to her faithful. While the Queen was busy distributing the wealth of her unfortunate subjects, Columbus was landing in an unknown world, in a new continent, the wrong continent they didn't know had existed. By the time he came back the Queen had cleaned out all the undesirable subjects, meaning the Jews, Muslims, Gypsies and anyone else who didn't think like her ideas and ways of beliefs, anyone who did not accept Christianity. By getting rid of the prosperous and healthy society of the Jews and Muslims and the rest of the non-Christian society, who were after all productive and well educated people of her country, in her blindness and hatred and ignorance, she opened the wound which has not been healed even today, not knowing the consequences or gains created by her actions.

I would think that by doing what she had done, throwing out of the country massive numbers of citizens, she created an open door for all the citizens who accepted her ideals of pure Roman Christianity. Homes and businesses left behind obviously must have been given to the people who didn't have anything as a reward for their support of her government. But she did not know, neither I believe did she think, that history would remember the religious symbols, and mosques and synagogues would survive as historical monuments to remind us that once integrated society will prosper more profoundly and become morally aware and compassionate. It's almost sad to think that any society or individual group of people believe they can be better off by themselves than as part of a community. Even nature does not allow that in her plans and flowers. If there is no wind to blow the pollen from one plant to the other, or bees to dig their feet inside the flowers to deposit their pollen without knowing, only the instinct of nature to do it, we would never be able to enjoy the beauty of flowers that we see in our own gardens and everywhere around us.

I have had the pleasure to visit Alhambra, and Granada, and to see all the Islamic historical places. There was no music playing. There was no belly dancer dancing. There were no Arabian horses prancing, and no mothers and fathers calling their children to a dinner table. There were only empty walls with mosaics that recorded the history and the wonderful culture, history which has been silent for almost five hundred years. I ask myself, is Spain better off today without the wonderful citizens who were forced to leave their beautiful homeland? I would say with confidence, "No, they are not better off without them." There is much that is missing in the mosaic of empty spaces in today's Spain. Like everything else, life begins in one place and ends exactly in the same. It begins in Mother Earth and it goes right back to it. Looking back in history, a profound impact in the world had happened by the single action of the Queen of Spain granting Columbus the necessary finances to take the trip. That has profoundly changed the course of history and the world. Spain became a most powerful country by the wealth for the short period of time and the biggest crusader to spread Christianity, not by inspiring people to convert through faith, nor even by bribing people with financial and material gifts, but by the way of the blade of the sharp sword. So who has any right to say that Islam is a religion of the sword? America was neither a Christian nor Islamic continent. There were millions of native people, well advanced civilizations, perhaps even more civilized than the men from Europe who had come and conquered them and converted them forcefully to a God they had never known.

Many new oppressive countries have been created in the five hundred years since European man landed on this continent, but there is only a very short time with a history of free people, only one country the freedom was born in, and that is my country the United States of America. It is clear to me that many of the great industrialists who took part in the subjection and development of the Arabian lands were sincere about wanting to give the local people genuine freedom and to enable them to progress with the West. So the two hands of the conquest, one hand giving and support, one hand taking and controlling, worked together for better or for worse.

The greedy and the oppressor will employ power that no one can oppose, and then put into authority local tribal leaders who will enforce rule in return for their position. There is nothing very esoteric or secret about that. The trans-continental land of Jordan, the valley of Babylon, and the high desert of Saudi Arabia, from the shores of the Red Sea to the Indian Ocean, was divided up into regions that could not alone offer resistance to modern military technology, and each was put into the hands of those local influential families who would agree to the right mineral development projects. Such leaders characteristically do not care about the masses of their people, and those leaders certainly did not understand the nature of the wealth they were sitting upon.

With the money they began to receive from the sale of the oil the West agreed was theirs, the new leaders of the Arabic countries purchased the mechanical advantages of the Industrial Revolution for themselves. They bought the highways, the steel tower cities, and the automobiles. But because they did not adopt with them the culture of the nations that created those things, in fact even rebuked that culture as evil and corrupt, a certain cultural neurosis was created among them. When one of the first of the new Princes was given as a gift by European colonizers a strange two-wheeled bicycle, the young man is reported to have asked his servants to bring some food in a bowl, and to place it beside the bicycle so that the machine might prove to be an angel and not a devil or a demon, as demonstrated by whether or not the rider is thrown to the ground. It might have been the same sort of good luck gesture as leaving a plate of cookies out for Santa Claus, but it reflected how they felt about the whole world the West represented. It became very problematical for them to deal with the worldly success of the West, when Westerners do exactly the things that their own religion declares to be evil. Even if they can buy the fruits of Western success, they shall always be bitter fruits for them, for it is not those fruits they desire so much as to be successful themselves, and so to prove the righteousness of their own culture and religion. They want to beat the West at its own game, but to do so without behaving in accordance with its values, or succumbing to lust for its prizes.

Their feelings of discomfort were not made less by the apparent ability of another player in the area to play the West's game very well. In the land where Christ was born and known as a man of peace, the land had been covered with blood since long before he was crucified. It was a land of jealous and bloodthirsty gods at war, a land where new religions were born, Zoroastrianism, the sacred writings based on the concept of a conflict between a spirit of good and evil, Orthodoxy, Catholicism, Christianity and also Islam, religions that should only focus on the spirit of light and good and not of darkness and evil. Schisms between the churches in Constantinople and Rome, and between them and Mecca, caused great hardship to the relatively small community of people who had so long lived in the valley of the Jordan River, the Hebrew and Jewish communities. They were hardly the proprietors of the place. After the war with the Romans, and the rise of Christianity and Islam, they had been oppressed, enslaved, at best tolerated, and dispersed around the world for two thousand years. More than anything else, the Jewish people everywhere dreamed of coming back home to Judea.

History has said Moses tried to take his people from Egypt into Israel, a place that had seen much shedding of blood since long before he arrived there. The legend tells that Moses was not successful in finally bringing his people home. Then in 1948, the journey seemed finally to come to an end, the journey of the second coming to the Promised Land.

From the point of view of the local Muslim and Christian population, the creation of the state of Israel was like seeing a genie rising from a bottle that had been lost in the desert for many centuries. Suddenly the genie realized that he was free from the confinement of his world in the little bottle. Finally he had seen the light of hope, and there was no turning back. This was his chance and the only chance to become a nation, and with the good intentions of some good people and neighbors over the ocean, the dream became real. The genie is here and here to stay. Self-imprisonment or self-exile serves no purpose, a repeat for the exile of the Jewish people. The right of their existence after all is justified, by all means. Because of their own persecution, the Jews at times have been unkind and revengeful towards their neighbors, Christians and Muslims. Perhaps they didn't know any better or they thought it was the right thing to do to be unkind to your own neighbor and fellow man. They have had new wounds during World War II echoing in their minds and souls, their grandparents and parents, brothers and sisters dying from starvation and in the gas chambers in the millions in very inhumane ways. None of us lifted a hand to try and save them from the tragedy that was happening, the only time we intervened is when our existence was threatened by the butchery of Nazism and fascism in Europe. Then the Christian and Muslims pretended to be the saviors of the chosen children of Abraham but they were the ones who were killing and gassing them and trying to exterminate them just the day before and ignoring their cries. We may all be guilty of many things, but I truly believe that in the eyes and heart of our supreme being, whoever He may be, universe or a living God, we always remain innocent in his eyes and heart. He may see us as incompetent and not understanding the consequences of our deeds.

In the new land of America, the Muslim religion was almost unheard of, in other words it was an alien thing. Pure Christianity was divided into many different groups, Protestants of a dozen sects, Catholic and Orthodox, and the newest and most radical, the strangely spiritual fanatics calling themselves born again Christians. In the early sixties there were turbulent times, the Vietnam war, Woodstock and the Beatles, hippies, and finally an introduction of that alien religion of Islam in America. Imam Mohamed and his radical follower Louis Fahrakan rose to power and influence in the black community, and likewise the passionate and peace loving young Malcolm X, a promising leader who unfortunately didn't live long enough to present Islam to a black and white America. In Dr. Martin Luther King, Jr., America discovered another leader who tried to preach peace and equality to all mankind, regardless of race, color, or religion. The unfortunate death of this African-American man perhaps more than any other has given us more awareness of how we should treat each other as fellow human beings. Their deaths have not gone in vain, for as President John F. Kennedy said, "Ask not what your country can do for you, but what you can do for your country." The words are profound and very heavy even today, and they define what it means to be a patriot.

ABOUT THE RELIGION

Recorded history has such a short journey. Whatever happened before? Who is to say the world was not much better or more advanced than it is today? I am sitting comfortably behind the desk of my computer and trying to make sense of my emotions, going deep in my soul and calling inside myself out loud. It's almost as people used to do in ancient times, calling from hill to hill with loud echoing voices to pass the messages or deliver the news. And now I want to call inside of myself to my heart and my soul, "Hello my friend, do you know me? Can you tell me anything about yourself? Can you tell me what we have been all these eternal years?"

I get no response. Neither my soul nor emotions take me any farther than what has been written and recorded by our ancestors. Even the most ancient prophecies that have been written are as young as the dew in morning from the long night rain. Our ancestors traveled long distance with harsh conditions at times to unknown worlds just as we do today. One can imagine having no instruments to read a distance or to guide, no roads, just a journey to the unknown places and environments. With each step the danger and sickness for them and their families must be difficult to imagine. Encountering perhaps native tribes and villages who were afraid for their own territorial instinct to protect as in human nature. Each destination of each tribe, whenever they had moved, there must have been significant losses of life. Perhaps not being well adapted to the climate or the hostility of the natural environment and the species that lived in each area of the new settlements, each day was a fight to survive and each day I believe made them stronger and more experienced for the next journey to be safer and easier. In their struggle and understanding of the love of life and their families and going far and beyond to the unknown to provide a better life for themselves and their families, they became in a way explorers, as we have done now and our forefathers before us. Their will to survive should be cheered as a success because we are here. They have triumphed to preserve human life. Each generation has taken new steps with new understanding and vision, and exploration for the good of all men. As well as the struggle of our ancestors to find new lands they also had to contend with the earth and her natural sicknesses. I try to make sense of the evolution and the turmoil that mother earth has gone through in the last ten million years. She has gone mad and exploded with temper with volcanoes and then got sick, throwing up her ashes over most of the planet wiping out most of the species but somehow we are still here and at times she's been kind to us providing us with everything we need to build shelters to become what we are today. She would go to sleep and let herself recoup. Perhaps we are all only a dream which will pass away when she awakens again.

The island of Crete in the heart of the Mediterranean, was that once part of the main land? Was it once part of the Atlantis civilization, or was all of that only a fairy tale story? No one can really answer that question. I will only say that I could comfortably look and feel at home when I see the landscape of the Caspian Sea and the Black Sea and the lush green valley of the Danube River. I will close my eyes and dream and wonder and imagine in any shape or form how it could be, what it was really like then when the Caspian Sea and the Pontus Euxinus were not there. There were only streams and lush valleys with children playing and the mothers and fathers trying to provide for their families and the Kings preparing the armies trying to protect their villages and towns from invaders. If I could just drift in that wonderland over the last two million years, maybe I would find myself in not much of a different world than I am living today. Two million years is an astronomical time for any creature that lived on the planet. If we are talking about the galaxy's time then two million years is the blink of an eye. What could such a length of time mean to me, and to the world as I know it?

Every religion I know of is based on teaching me that I am something more than just the body and the role I occupy during this brief instant in time I know as my life. If I do possess an immortal soul, then does not all of time become important to me? If I believe that, then it becomes important to me to observe the movement of history, and to take steps to make our future as beautiful a place to live as possible, if not for ourselves then for other souls.

I believe all religion is a way of seeking some reality to explain that feeling that we know we are something more than just the mortals we appear to be today. I believe something very real and very true lies behind all of the images we create when we try to describe the One we call God. These images, these religions, are like maps written in symbol, and as I know that no map actually is the journey it describes, I believe we can each find God, no matter if we have any one religion or another. As someone once said, all roads lead to Rome, and I want to say all religions lead to God if you search for God with an open heart.

Unfortunately, most of the millions of people in history have not agreed with me about that, and they have taken the teachings of their religions to set themselves apart from those who do not use the same map to God, who do not seek the same name of God. This has placed mankind in a battle against itself for almost all of the recorded history we have. In fact, much of our recorded history is nothing more than the ancient books of those religions, and their accounts of fighting people from other religions.

We have learned so much in the last five centuries about our world and about our history, and about each other, that a reasonable person might expect if people found disagreement among the different versions of any of the religious "maps" which have grown out of those obscure beginnings of literate history, then we would acknowledge their origins and quickly come to agreement on their fundamental common truths. Unfortunately, this has not happened, and we now stand on the threshold of a world war among people armed with nuclear and biological weapons, fighting over the smallest details of their religions. Such a fight is a blasphemy of everything all of us claim to believe in.

Be not deceived. The terrible wars and massacres and injustices of the Middle East, like those in the Balkan states, are not about oil, or political regimes, or settlements. They are at root the direct effect of the religious bigotry that leads people to persecute people who are not of their own religion. The oil, the regimes, the settlements, and the like are only the cards and chips in the game, but the game is being played among people who do feel that way about their religions. Each claims to be acting in the name of God, and doing what God commands them to do.

These are people who have convinced themselves that the prophecies are about themselves, and they must be the ones who fulfill the prophecies to prove their version of the story is truer than the others. What is most tragic is that the religions in conflict are all factions of believers of one common story about the relationship between God and mankind, as revealed to a man named Abraham. They each claim to worship God. Sadly, they each believe that same God loves only one of them, and each is ready to kill the others to prove himself the true heir after all.

My Christian friends point out to me the truth that their religion is one of compassion, tolerance, and forgiveness, calling for a life of honest treatment of all one's brethren. It is not, they insist, about judging, and the persecution of the sinner and the unsaved. My Jewish friends point out to me the truth that their religion is likewise one of just law, and honest treatment of all, not of obsession with guilt. Likewise I point out to them that the Islam I know and love is a call to compassion for all life, and a call to live a clean and virtuous life, and certainly not a cult of wild homicidal fanatics. There is nothing about Islam itself that would lead Muslims to see Americans, or any other such people, as demons of Satan that must be destroyed.

Yet today a three-headed hydra stands on the Arabian Peninsula, and each head is armed with weapons that can kill the whole beast, each prepared to kill the other two. Each of them claims to be the sole heir to the earthly estate of the same God. Each of them wears the crown of some state or another.

As a Muslim in America, even if one for whom it is a religion I love, but not a ritual practice, I find myself more and more troubled about the villain role into which Americans are increasingly casting Muslims. I feel more and more helpless to do anything to show that my being a Muslim does not in any way dampen my great sense of patriotism and love for this country, my country. One of the many reasons I love America so much is that a man can be a Muslim and a patriot here, and stand shoulder to shoulder with Christians and Jews who feel the same way. I find myself frightened when I think about the German patriots of the 1930's who suddenly found themselves cast as villains and traitors because they were Jewish. What could they do besides protest? "We are German, we are patriots, and we have supported the German state in peace and war." It did not matter. The truth did not matter. Only that they were Jews mattered.

What can I do? I am an American, I am a patriot, and I have supported the United States of America in peace and in war.

I am not an Arab Muslim, as if such a distinction makes a difference, but a Bosnian Muslim. In my efforts to help my ancestral people in Bosnia, I became a valuable asset to my government in Washington in its efforts to bring stability to Bosnia, and to protect the security of all of the different factions and ethnic groups which make up a tapestry of that troubled Balkan region. I can't claim to have been an American James Bond, but I can feel proud to say I was his friend. More about that later, but it doesn't change the way people are going to treat me now.

I wonder how many people thought the title of this book was some kind of oxymoron? Does the rest of America honestly believe there is no such thing as a Muslim American patriot? If Americans now fear that every American Jew is really a patriotic Israeli in the closet, then to whom do they think we Muslims are loyal, "Osama Da Bomba" who has murdered my countrymen, or the leaders of hostile Muslim nations? Have we reached the point where Americans believe there is something about the Islamic faith that just naturally makes us into screaming fanatical homicidal terrorists, each of us just waiting for that mad moment when we take up the scimitar and go chasing our neighbors' children?

What can I do? At best I can tell what I have done, what I think, and what I feel. I am a Muslim American patriot. I have written to challenge other Muslim Americans to stand up and make your patriotism clear to everyone. We are not the enemy. We are an important group of Americans, and we should make that clear to everyone.

I have no doubt that with this book I shall offend some, perhaps with my outspoken opinions, or with my limited knowledge of history and religion, or with the things I have done. I seek to insult or offend no one, but hope only to exhort all to find in their faith the wisdom and strength to put aside the petty quarrels of sectarianism and bigotry, and seek the common goals of peace, health, and a virtuous life which all of our religions promote.

ABOUT A BIRTHDAY PARTY

I once attended a birthday party in Las Vegas, at the sumptuous home of one of the city's most prominent Jewish businessmen and leaders, a man I shall simply call Shell. I was very privileged to have been invited to his son's fourth birthday party, attended by a grand assortment of people including the great midnight idol Wayne Newton, who happened to be a friend of mine as well. Some were noted Israeli politicians and businessmen, including a noted political editorial writer from The Jerusalem Post. At that particular time there was a domestic terrorist bombing in a Jewish neighborhood in Buenos Aires. Many people were hurt, and it was the subject of much conversation at the party.

I observed and listened to the reactions of the people throughout the room. Even though no Muslims were known to be involved, I was amazed to hear such a negative and cold tone in their speculations about who had done it. I would have expected more sorrow for the victims, and less hate and anger toward all of Argentina as a nation. I even heard such phrases as, "Those hopeless miserable people, between the terrorists and the Nazis, I wish they were on our borders so we could pay them back for everything they have done." They talked about the strength of Israel, and the pursuit of anti-Semitic war criminals in South America. During their conversation, it crossed my mind to wonder if they were ever going to mention the United States as the country that has been the big brother and greatest supporter of Israel.

There were more than twenty tables in the birthday party room. I will not say the name of the boy because I will respect his privacy, so I will call him Madison. The names that I saw on the name cards of each table were not names of the guests, nor even of the places they came from. Instead they were the names of Biblical heroes and historic places in today's Israel. Considering, I assumed, that Madison enjoyed the great benefits of dual citizenship, and was living in one of the most opulent places in all of America, I would have expected to see perhaps a few American landmarks also. I might have expected to hear Madison being told of some of the American heroes, especially the ones who have made it possible for Israel to be what it is today. There was talk about Europe, none of it expressing the least love for it with the exception of England. I got the impression that if they ever could feel certain to be successful, they would put Europe in one huge cannon shell and send her on a one way trip to a faraway galaxy, with no regrets from those distinguished gentlemen at that innocent beautiful boy's birthday party.

I held him in my arms and hugged him gently and sincerely and kissed his cheek and wished him a happy birthday as my own child. Truthful love from my heart and in my eyes his mother and father have seen, and I have blushed with their kindness and respect for me. The boy's mother is Israeli born, highly intelligent and presents herself with confidence, and even though she is very physically small in appearance she seems tall and I'm sure in her heart feels tall, she's soft spoken, almost shy. She is very beautiful in mind, heart, and soul, definitely a wonderful mother that any child would be fortunate to have. His father Shell is the son of a Boston taxi driver, and he has built a fortune in this great country of the United States, and has become an international multi-billionaire. People listen when he speaks. I told him I believe that immigrants like ourselves, both Jewish and Muslim, should be more grateful to the nation that has given us everything. I hope Shell is grateful, and hasn't forgotten that this nation has made him what he is today.

"Does the boy like music?" I asked him. "My children like classical music."

The boy's mother replied with a big smile on her face, "We listen to nothing but classical music, would you care for me to name them all for you?"

I laughed and said, "No please, let me guess, please, maybe we have at least one more thing in common." I mentioned many of the classical legends. We both laughed and she said she believes that classical music enhances intelligence in youngsters. In her heavy Hebrew accent, she asked me what kind of music I like. I told her that I was a rock and roll boy from the sixties, and that I got in a lot of trouble for it, as Tito didn't approve of rock music.

Shell agreed the sixties were revolutionary and troublesome times. "Vietnam was surely a sad chapter in American history," he said. "President Johnson wasn't thinking of what he was getting into. So many of our children have died and the wounds are still fresh in our memories. We had demonstrations and killing on our campuses. To tell you the truth, for the first time in my life I was afraid for my country, although thank God, here we are in peace and prosperity."

I said, "Shell, you are a very fortunate man, and I am very honored to know you. One doesn't get to chat everyday with influential citizens such as you, sir. Your beautiful wife has told me…"

He cut me off and said, "She's a wonderful lady, she really does take good care of me. Angelo would you join me for a cup of coffee, since I was going to have one?" He asked as he gently, almost tiredly pushed himself up with his elbow on the chair.

I replied "I would be honored to pour a cup of coffee for us."

We walked shoulder to shoulder to his kitchen counter. I opened the cabinets as I was familiar with where the coffee cups were, pulled out two coffee mugs with the logo of the Star of David, and I recalled that he is the owner of one of the most famous hotels of Jerusalem.

I looked through the window while I was pouring coffee, and what I saw struck me like a blow. Across the pool stood a little house, where I saw a giant man with a black suit on, looking at the wall of the pool area, where two other men in overalls were cleaning and painting the wall. He was quite clearly a professional security officer of some kind. I might have guessed FBI.

"Is that man working for you, sir?" I asked.

He nodded his head and said softly, "Just last night, Angelo, some hateful people sprayed some graffiti inside the pool area on that wall. I wanted to have it cleaned and repainted before the party, but they were late."

I felt as if my heart dropped into my shoe. I felt compassion for his suffering, and then a sense of pity. It is easy to understand pity for someone because he is hungry or has no roof over his head, or because he couldn't buy a toy or new pair of shoes for his beautiful handsome boy. Such misfortune is easy to understand. It is not so easy to feel pity for any man who can buy and sell hotels, or jet planes, or ships like they were just furniture. I said, "Those bastards. What gives them the right to destroy something beautiful?"

"No, Angelo," he said, "It wasn't the destruction that I care about, but the threat to the safety of my family that worries me. They sprayed an iron cross all over the Star of David on those tile mosaics."

I finished pouring the coffee, put cream and two sugars, stirred the coffee, his and mine gently, and walked towards his table. I put my hand on his left shoulder gently and told him, "Shell, here's your coffee, my friend."

He looked at me with his old and tired face, and said, "Thank you Angelo." What a poignant moment that was for me as I brought our coffee to the table and placed his cup in front of him. A powerful and accomplished man, with a huge influence, and there he was with me as vulnerable as any other human being, looking for comfort and assurance from another fellow man, something to assure him of hope. All the wealth that he has seems like really nothing to him at that moment.

I thought in my mind, "I wish that he sees everything across the Atlantic Ocean, far in the Middle East, where people are dying as we are speaking. A small country becomes a nuclear club member without admitting it to the rest of the world, with help from our government and the government of South Africa. The Israeli government is not too far from South Africa's idea of controlling troublesome elements of their population. Sometimes it seems like they're just testing their weapons. It is very unpleasant for me to think that my tax money and the influence of Shell's money have paid for many of those weapons that are killing so many Palestinians and Israelis as well. There is no doubt that statistics show that there is no family on either side, Israeli or Palestinian, that has not been effected by that, and suffered the loss of loved ones.

Some of his guests were already asking the questions that one would expect. Have you called the police? Have they done anything about it? The way they were asking, their body language, however, struck me like they really didn't care much about it, even though they were expected to express a certain outrage about it. It was as though they were just asking for the sake of asking, as if such things as that are happening all the time and are hardly more than a nuisance. Perhaps they felt they would like to express much more, but were expected to maintain a certain polite nonchalance. It was very surreal to me, unpleasantly moving to see them so out of touch with humanity. These were good people, successful people, influential people who felt good about showing off their cashmere clothing and Armani colognes. I am not a millionaire, but I own cashmere also and think nothing of it. I buy it because the feeling is good on my body, not because it means something. I was sadly moved to hope to see them come down to earth, and not to look as if they were above all the suffering and the turbulent lives of the rest of the people.

I listened to the guests chat on about politics and business, and listened to them as they spoke to Shell before leaving. "Nice party Shell," they said, but there was no mention of the little boy Madison. Nice party. There were no thanks, just a fast few political expressions again, exchanges between them. When I left I spoke to Shell's wife and she gave me a big hug and thanked me for helping to make the party a success. I made my apologies and slipped out without bothering Shell with farewell amenities.

I could not stop thinking about that party. When I look at the turbulence and killing in the Middle East on the front pages of newspapers, I think of the people I met at the birthday party. Why do they not do something to stop it? I could not get over how a little boy's birthday and his innocence and celebration of his life for a better tomorrow had become a political gathering, and how casually so many of the guests were able to express a very bitter hatred toward so much of the world they live in. How can I or anyone sleep in peace, knowing that such influential people all around the world are sitting, drinking coffee, and thinking, "How can I chop up the planet into little pieces, like a baked Alaskan ice cream pie? I eat the pie, and what I don't eat, I can put it in a cannon shell and send it to the far galaxies so that no one else can have a piece of it." Do I think that's selfish or greedy or maybe evil? That would be easy to say, but I think the truth is it is neither one of them. It's only our human nature that has taught us to protect our individual territory as any other species on our beautiful planet.

These are not crass avaricious villains, cackling in materialistic lust for gold, they are good people who are responsible to various organizations and movements, who celebrate birthdays and Bar Mitzvahs and baptisms, and whose children go to school. Would a four-year-old little Jewish boy feel any different on his birthday than a four-year-old Muslim or any other boy? In a word, they are not "they" so much as they are "we." Does worldly power of one father, or the poverty of another father, impress a four year old boy, or is he more moved by how his father cares for him and embraces him?

Today in the twenty first century we are capable of sending everything to hell. No need to look to the cannon shell and the far galaxy. Why do we feel so much hatred and misunderstanding towards each other? Was the conflict of pride and greed that is told of in the story of Cain and Abel simply an expression of unchangeable human nature? Are we simply cursed by God because of that unfortunate time in pre-history?

I cannot accept that. I must believe that God has not placed that in our path as a condition of our existence, but instead as an obstacle to surmount, and to grow beyond. We must get off the thinking that there is no way out. Perhaps we do possess eternal souls, and our life is an eternal journey, but all things and conditions in the world change and pass. Where there is the beginning, there is always an end, and in every end, there is always a beginning. So I do have hope for us humans. We are always capable of more loving and caring than hating. I hope that my little friend Madison's birthday party will be something that he remembers warmly, and I look forward to see the day when the honest brokers and the representatives will use their good offices to truly represent their people in the way that crying mothers would wish them to on behalf of all the four year olds in the world.

Today in the 21st Century, Israel is a real nation offering a real home to all of Judaism. For all of its problems, and for all of its offenses, it has survived the experiment that created it in 1948, and it has become a nation of world-class power, to be recognized and reckoned with. What a fine and wonderful thing that is. Israel is a very tiny nation in body, if we consider only the Middle Eastern real estate it occupies. When we consider that it is the focus of an international network of Israeli citizens abroad and of millions of supporters of many nationalities, we see that Israel is very big in heart, and has a possibility for a promise of a great future. Lacking or missing is only one thing. They have not learned to love and accept their neighbors.

They must rid themselves of the bitterness that comes from seeing themselves as chronically victimized people. They must rid themselves of whatever gain they perceive in the passive aggressive manipulation of guilt to win power by making themselves a victimized people, so as to exploit the sympathy of seekers of justice. It is the unfortunate consequence of this hypocrisy not only that it leads them to a certain self-destructive masochism, but that it leads them to see other people as being either their opponents in litigation or chumps on the jury. The unfortunate consequence of this is that other people will find such behavior supportive of the stereotype of the separatist predatory Jew, which cruel misperception serves the good of no one.

My point is that Shell is an honorable American deserving respect, and Israel is for all its troubles an honorable country, and Shell's love for Israel is fine, but I believe that in general the immigrant American Jews should feel and show a great deal more gratitude to this country than they do.

IT'S NOT EASY BEING JEWISH EITHER

My family's homeland, Bosnia, has been a safe haven for Jewish people from the year 711 to 1492, hundreds of years, the Jewish people have been members of our family, even given that Bosnia was of almost one hundred percent Islamic faith at that time. My forefathers have offered shelter, genuine human friendship, and neighborly goodness from their heart. They have protected and treated the Hebrews with respect and dignity, helped them build the neighborhoods and synagogues, and opened the way for their participation in the society and the community as equals for more than seven centuries.

In all ways we are all children of one God and He hears all our prayers in the same sentences. I find it ironic when I look back and I know that before I was born, a madman in Europe tried to eliminate an entire race of people. Even then they were received with open arms, and they could find protection for their families. In Turkey since the beginning of the Ottoman Empire until today, the Jewish faith people flourished in every way and lived with the freedom and respect and dignity of free people all through the empire. Today in the beginning of the 21st Century, however, I should honestly state that my forefathers and my religion Islam have not lately been seen as protectors of the Jewish people.

Since 1948, since the creation state of Israel, my religion has suffered a blow as evil, dirty, unmerciful, unforgiving, and uncompassionate as any that has been done by propaganda and deliberate hatred. I will not call it done by the Zionists, as I believe that it was not done by the deliberate intention of anyone, but seems to be the cumulative result of many good intentions taken too far. It is natural to understand that there will be hostile repercussions from the centuries of alienation, and from the recent decades of outright persecution. It is natural to understand the intentions of the Israeli government and their revolutionary forefathers, from David Ben Gurion to Menachem Begin to Moshe Dayan. My favorite among those who rose up from the ashes of the millions of corpses to create the Phoenix that is Israel is the American born teacher, Prime Minister Golda Mier.

What a fantastic lady she was, a wonderful mother, a wonderful teacher, a wonderful leader.

Others, of course, are not such charitable persons as Meir, and have more reflected the righteous seeming rage of having been an oppressed people, like Sherman Perez, a Palestine born Jew filled with resentment and hatred for large portions of mankind, and the security state extremist, former General Ariel Sharon, today's Prime Minister who I personally think should be tried for the suffering and killing of the Palestinian women and children and equally Israeli women and children who have been the victims of his misrepresentation and ignorance. A man blinded by hatred towards his neighbors, the Palestinians, and equal blindness of the Palestinians towards the Israelis. Sharon has a hate with no hope for remorse and should never be in the position of the authority that he commands. If I were in his neighborhood I would certainly not sleep soundly. During the Israeli and Egyptian war in 1962, under his command, with his orders as a commander of his battalion or his brigade, Egyptian men women and children were found praying in the Mosques. They were gunned down when they were kneeling and praying to God for peace, not just for peace of their own, but their neighbors as well, the Israelis.

Another brutal and unprovoked murder was committed when our spy ship, Liberty was in the Egyptian waters during the war. Israeli air force and navy clearly knew that was an American vessel. I remember as a child, Marshall Tito of Yugoslavia told my uncle who was then a General and one of the staff members in Tito's cabinet and with loud laughing they talked about the incident that happened to the Liberty. Tito had said, "Can't you see the Israeli's propaganda is absolutely fantastic? They are hoping that Americans will think the Russians have sunk the Liberty." Fortunately the ship did not sink, but survived because of the will and the love for life of the American navy men.

President Tito was quoted in saying President Nasser of Egypt had called him personally and asked him for assurance from Russia that if he wins the war against Israel that America will not attack. Tito had responded sarcastically and with and mocking laughter and said that he needed to go to Egypt the next morning to deliver the message to Nasser from Kremlin Soviet Union. He did go to Egypt and gave Nasser the news, that news that he wished he never heard. It almost reminds me of the history of the Alamo and Daniel Boone waiting for help that never arrived. Tito delivered the news that the Russians are not coming, that they are not interested in a confrontation with America. Privately they told Tito that Nasser and all his government entourage are not worthy to be protected from Israeli invasion. Nasser should be able to take care of Israel by himself, like he said.

We all know what happened. Israeli superiority was unsurpassed militarily. They even crossed the Suez Canal. I don't understand why they didn't go to Cairo to have a coffee or to say hello to Nasser at his palace. That sure would be a monumental moment, but this was pretty good, what already had been done. It seems like then the United States government had realized that Israel was worthy to be an ally of ours. We have offered money, military hardware, even a nuclear bomb. Kennedy's administration didn't acknowledge the word "can't. Anything or everything that Israel needed, it was provided by the Kennedy administration. I can agree with everything that has been given to Israel but one thing. Allowing her to be a nuclear power makes many neighbors nervous and does not make Israel any safer. I don't mean nervous from her Arab neighbors, there is really nothing they can do about it anyway. The nervous neighbors are across the Mediterranean. Earlier in 1941, France, Germany, Italy, Romania, Russia, Poland, and all of Europe with the exemption of Turkey, they were all down each other's throat trying to exterminate one another by any means. The Jews got caught up in the middle and they paid a heavy price. Europe and Russia I think seriously have a bone to pick with Israel today. Does anybody really think that Israel wouldn't like to pick up a baseball bat and remind Europe of being bad boys and not caring for all their citizens? Forgiven maybe but definitely not forgotten. So don't go to sleep and think you can wake up safe and sound in the morning. So if you owe someone something better think about how you should pay them back without them coming to collect. It seems like common sense to me.

Before and after World War II, in the creation of the trans-continental Jordan countries, many kingdoms and states were formed without any particular justification, some of them so small they were little more than a single powerful family's local compound, but very strategically located with respect to their natural resources. When Israel was founded, it is estimated there were less than one hundred thousand Hebrews living there. In only a few years, the number of Jewish people coming from Europe to the land that was promised to them through Abraham was over a million. They were simply inundated with refugees from all over the world. With the British and the United Nations willing to help organize Jewish defense and the creation of Israel, the legitimacy of their property claims was, whether righteous or not, uncontestable.

At the same time the French and British were having problems all through their colonies in the Middle East. Each time they lost a colony, they became more resentful towards Islam and the Muslim people. England and France lost Syria,

Lebanon, Egypt, and the areas including the Suez Canal, and these losses were hard to swallow. They came to believe it was the religion, and not the social conditions of occupation, which led the Muslim people to oppose them. As a result, many good and peace loving people suffered the pride of the murderous hired killers of the so-called elite force of the French Foreign Legion.

Like some of the ancient Janissaries of the Ottoman time, this was a kind of dark monastic cult made up of volunteers from the losers and dregs from all over the globe, men of every land and color who had no ties to anyone, and no loyalty but to their own corps. These had no love or mercy for anyone, and as such shock troops always seem to do, they were raping women and children and mercilessly killing defenseless people throughout the French colonies. They were good at losing every military battle, whether with the guerrillas or a regular army.

The English on the other hand were moral colonizers, using the iron will of their leaders and the iron fists of their troops to create discipline. Losing Egypt had been a blow to their pride. These were two old rivals, each a true enemy of the other. The French have never got any respect from the English, and they have lost every war they have fought with England, from Napoleon in Brittany to the loss of Quebec in Canada. How ironic that they teamed up when they needed each other. The one opportunity they had to stand together in opposition to the forces of Islam, as they perceived them, was to support the establishment of a specifically non-Islamic political state in the region. Israel provided for them a foothold for control of the region, in a sense making the political move a kind of crusade.

Recognition of Israel as a sovereign State brought on war to almost all of the Arab states, Syria, Jordan, Lebanon, Egypt, Sudan, Libya, and other surrounding countries. They took the creation of Israel as a betrayal toward all of Middle Eastern world. In 1912, the Ottoman Empire was defeated and brought back to their original borders, now named Turkey. Middle Eastern countries participated in helping the allied countries to contain the forces of young Turkish leader Kemal Ataturk. His words echo even today the words of one of his generals, Jafer Pasha Koljenovic, that the Muslim world in the Middle East has become seedless. There are no young trees to bear fruit at the end of the season, which means in ancient expressions that the people have not grown the leaders to lead them to a better future.

When Nasser and his entourage of uneducated generals and their untrained army were given a resounding defeat by Israel's Jewish defense force, most of the world was surprised. When the Egyptian government blocked the Suez Canal from any ship entering, France and England both armed Israel up to the teeth.

There was overnight a change of heart among the Europeans and the Americans and the Jewish people all around the world. Seemed like everyone had forgotten who it was had saved and given the Jewish people a safe haven for millenniums from all their tragedy and torment up until 1948 and the creation of Israel. It was the Muslim world. Suddenly the Muslim religion became the biggest enemy of the Jewish faith and the Jewish people. I will argue that some people have short memories.

Islam is not an enemy of the Jewish people. I myself have been always supportive of the Jewish people and to their cause. Their fight was just and is morally right to survive, but it is still not just that they should do so at the expense of other human beings. At this time Arab Palestinian people are genuine victims, caught in a cross fire between European capitalist interests and a conflict of religious ideology which really serves no one. During the Arab-Israeli war in 1962 some Egyptian forces reached the walls of Jerusalem. Indiscriminate bombing of the citizens of Jerusalem by the fanatic Nasser's army brought hardship equally to the Palestinians and Jews. But the reaction of the government of Israel brought even greater hardship to the Palestinians, who were blamed for Nasser's crimes because they were Muslims.

The Israeli Army, sophisticated and well trained, had given an astonishing blow of defeat to the Egyptian Arab union army. That sweeping victory also produced a mass exodus of the Palestinian people, who departed to escape persecution or were forcefully thrown out of their land and homes. The Palestinian exodus created a leadership under the then young and charismatic Yasser Arafat, in exile for the first time in Palestinian history inside or outside of Palestine. Nasser promised them they would be back to Palestine, although the promise was never delivered, he even lost the battle of the Sinai Peninsula to Israeli forces all the way to the Suez Canal. It looked like the promise to return to the West Bank and Gaza had been doomed. For a second time in history it looked like Abraham needed to bring two cousins together, Palestinians and Hebrews to give them a second chance in life. This time it will not be Cyrus the Great, it will be the United States of America, the only broker. The Hebrews and Palestinians were taken to the promised land by Abraham who left the city of Ur in what is today Iraq, thousands of years before Christ, Moses, and Mohammed. If they want to call themselves children of Abraham, Moses or Mohammed, I could argue that Moses and Mohammed should call themselves children of Palestinian and Hebrew descendants.

Palestinian leader Yasser Arafat, a diehard patriot of his people for his people, became radical and irrational in his decisions of how to bring about the recognition and justice the Palestinians rightfully deserved. Arafat realized he was not getting any help from his cousin Jordan. Instead he got thrown out of Jordan on a one-way trip through Syria to Lebanon. On the so-called Black September, a brutal fight between Palestinian and Jordanian forces took place and left thousands of dead, wounded and displaced Palestinian people with no place to go. Some arrangements were made with the Syrian and Lebanese governments that Palestinian refugees could go to Lebanon. That was the beginning of the tragic saga of the terrorist suicide bombings, all the blessings of Yasser Arafat. Since then there has been no peace or security inside Israel and the occupied territories, Gaza and the West Bank and the rest of the world.

In the meantime Israelis were developing and perfecting security measures they could only have learned in their experience during Hitler's torture of the Jews. Now they are starting to use almost the same tactics of brutality, torture, forceful eviction, confiscating of homes, businesses and properties, and of course, the endless arrests and shooting of unarmed people who were throwing rocks and receiving bullets back. Because of the paranoia and insecurity of the Israeli government, perhaps unintentionally, they started to use the same methods of persecution like that of Nazi Germany. Now they are branding people with their special license plates for identity as Palestinians, just like Nazis did to the Jews, branding them with tattoos and serial numbers. Bulldozing Palestinian homes, and beating and imprisoning Palestinian people has done more than any agitator could to inflame young boys who today become suicide bombers without mercy or regard for life.

Western media has a favorite myth that the suicide bombers all believe that if a Muslim blows himself away to kill an infidel or Israelis, that he will go in heaven and have twenty virgins or perhaps forty virgins. Well, let me correct anyone who thinks like that. I think that any person who is willing to give his or her life for the cause that they believe in, in a revolutionary way, who is fighting to free themselves from one they perceive to be an oppressor who has unjustly dominated their life, and who believes that their eternal soul will be blessed for it, has nothing to lose and has everything to gain. I believe that person, whoever they may be, truly does not care when they go to the mission of harming someone and themselves whether they are going to get one virgin or ten thousand. To be a suicide bomber and to be able to blow yourself up in a bus or a school or a restaurant, you must be very deeply convinced that you are doing what is of the highest moral value. When they do such things in the name of their nation, their race, or their religion, it becomes very difficult to say whether it is moral or immoral, as it is honored by many cultures. Were the Kamikaze pilots of Japan brainwashed psychopaths when they climbed into their Baka bombers and their miniature submarines to bomb Hawaii and to defend their homeland and their people from conquest? Did they kill themselves in massive numbers in suicide so that they will get one more virgin Geisha girl in heaven?

I call it tragic that any young boy or any young girl has to take their own life and someone else's with them to try to communicate a message of some kind, some desire to be heard, to win someone's compassion, attention or understanding. I think it is self-deluding however to think they are no more or less than fanatical psychopaths. To be willing even as a young person to voluntarily give up your life so that your people, and the ways of living and worshipping the God they treasure should survive is considered the height of heroism in America as well, as reflected in the words of Nathan Hale, "I regret that I have but one life to give for my country." It is terribly tragic, but it is hardly fair to call them evil, or insane.

In the meantime, all of this killing and kidnapping inside and outside Israel and Palestine has given the Christian world and enemies of the Middle Eastern world great justification for hostility toward both Israel and the Palestinians. It has been exploited particularly by the Israeli propaganda machine, which has been already in place and well perfected throughout the western world. All this time when the Muslim world is quarreling among each other about how to bring Palestinians back to their land, Israel found a new friend and ally in the United States of America.

Even before the close ties between Israel and the United States, Nasser's Egyptian government was given a lifetime opportunity to drop the idea of communism and so called Islamic socialism, and to drop becoming allied with the Soviet block. The United States basically promised to give Egypt any economical or military aid that they might desire. In his arrogance, President Nasser and his government brushed the United States off. Then Libya became a revolutionary state, and Colonel Kadafhi became President of Libya. He ordered the United States to move its military bases out of Libya. The American Jewish population started lobbying our politicians in Washington D.C. The Jewish population of the United States saw a golden opportunity of once in a lifetime to show our congress, senate and President that making Israel strong is equally in our best interest as well as the Israelis. The population which in the 1960's numbered three to four million, were well organized and well educated and integrated in American society one hundred percent. I look at it with amazement that from the end of World War II up to the mid-sixties the success of their integration in every aspect of American life, government, military, and private business, that it is really immeasurable. Everywhere you turn in America, the Jewish communities' hand has touched every aspect of life. Their vision for the survival of Israel has become true. They realized that this was their lifetime chance and perhaps only chance to safeguard and ensure the survival of Israel, and to convince the United States to support annexation of the occupied territories to enlarge Israel beyond its original borders. The Unites States was led to increase its influence in supporting Israel as an act to counter its losses in the region to the regimes in Egypt and Libya.

That was another blow that enraged the Middle East. It was no longer a war about Israelis and Arabs it was about Jews and Muslims. Now the page had turned. Palestinians were outraged that the actions of Libyans were used to justify oppressing them because they were both Muslims, which motivated more bombings, killings, and hijacking. News media no longer spoke only of Palestinian terrorists, but now of Muslim fanatics.

Some Christian organizations through the United States, led by men such as Pat Robertson, Jerry Falwell, and Jim Baker, allied their respective so-called born-again Christian organizations and with cooperation of some Jewish organizations created an unbreakable army of lobbyists through the Kennedy administration and beyond. Kennedy, not yet enough experienced at least in foreign affairs but good hearted, must have thought that the rights of Israel justified his support, but he forgot the rights of the Palestinians. Having very poor relations with the rest of the Middle Eastern countries, the Israeli lobbyists took every opportunity to strengthen the Israeli position as a military force. After all we were in a cold war with the Soviet Union, and we had no real allies in the Middle East. Kennedy realized that Israel could be a formidable ally in the region. As his predecessors had recognized it was the only place east of Greece for the U.S. to have a foothold in a non-Muslim country. Kennedy was willing to give monetary help in the order of two billion dollars a year for a population of not even three million Israelis.

The sudden awakening of Israel was like finding a bottle in the desert that was two thousand years old, and letting out the Genie that had been kept locked in it. When they pulled out the stopper, the Genie that came out was wearing the clothes of Uncle Sam, with the stars and stripes, and with an American Eagle protecting the Star of David and protecting the newborn state of Israel. Protecting it from what? From so-called terrorist threat of the Muslim world, as though Muslims had only been waiting their turn to follow in the footsteps of Hitler in persecuting Jews.

The Jewish community in the United States seized opportunities they have seen to be available in fact to any ethnic group, opportunity to take advantage of the political freedom that exists in our country. They invited many congressmen and senators to visit the newborn state of Israel, which was without question in a fight for survival. Every visitor or congressman who visited Israel was treated in profoundly cultural and traditional ways, which is unfortunately unknown to most of our people in America and the western world.

All of the Mediterranean Sea countries and the Balkan Peninsula have deep cultural traditions concerning visitors in their homes, and Jewish people are certainly a part of that heritage. When you are invited into their homes as guests, the atmosphere of respect for you as their guest is deeply engraved in culture and tradition with the most genuine expressions and gestures of warm hospitality. The Mediterranean people have won the hearts and minds of our many politicians every time one of them has visited Israel and they have come back with an experience of tradition which was really alien to them but something they liked and maybe thought they were missing at home. If one has never experienced such strong cultures, he or she will find it warm and tender as one can imagine. In that way during the Yom Kippur war, Prime Minister Golda Mair did not take our senators or congressmen to the halls of the Israeli government. No, she made sure that she took them to her house. She cooked for them and became for a moment the grandmother that our Senators never had or reminded them of the wonderful grandmothers they once had.

President Kennedy had a clear picture of the geopolitical situation in the twentieth century world. The Soviet Union with thousands of nuclear warheads could hit the United States at any place at any time. Having communist Cuba next door, for Kennedy and all the Presidents after him, it certainly is a small chicken bone in America's throat, a nuisance that we cannot live with. Kennedy was able to dominate the 1962 missile crisis and the crazy President Khrushchev, who had taken off his shoe at the UN and pounded it on the table. Sometimes a radical approach, if misunderstood, could bring unforgivable results. Thankfully, the Soviet leader was more rational than we believed, and backed down.

The United States has always and still is more willing and quicker to give and sell our military hardware to anyone who we assume are our friends and will listen to us, as long as we think it is in our national interest, economically or strategically and not thinking so much of the possible bad outcomes. The Soviet Union on the other hand was more reserved in spreading their nuclear or sophisticated military hardware outside the pact of the Soviet Union. Whereas the United States has given the opportunity and helped many countries to develop nuclear energy, including South Africa, India, Argentina, Chile, Brazil, and Iran, each of which has a nuclear research institute. We certainly had a hand in their nuclear development, for better or worse. Israel is the only country that does not belong to the nuclear club. They admit nothing, they agree to nothing, they promise nothing, and neither have they admitted or allowed any inspection from the nuclear commission from Vienna. During the development of the Israeli nuclear energy program, they proclaimed it was meant for the use of electricity, because they do not have any mineral resources to produce the electricity. It would of course be very naïve and unrealistic to believe that Israel does not possess a very sophisticated and varied nuclear arsenal, especially considering how many of the great scientists and engineers who discovered and developed nuclear power were Jewish refugees from Fascist Europe and Russia. So it goes.

The Chosen People sure haven't had much luck in returning to their promised land as peaceable inhabitants as Abraham and Moses had taught them. Even today, the chosen people are suffering hatred, bigotry, and discrimination. It is quite right that they should develop a resilient and strong will to survive. After two thousand years, the promise has not delivered peace and tranquility to Abraham's children. If it took two thousand years more, they would likely still be surviving. Times have changed, and some things have not changed, and I pray that times would change for the better, and I honestly mean that. I know from experience how hard it is to feel you are home, when you know in your heart that the place you call home is not really a safe place for you at all. I think that most Jewish people still feel like that, unsafe among their fellow human beings. It is not difficult to see a certain reaction to such feelings in observing how the powerful Genie of the state Israel has mastered how it should defend itself from its immortal enemies, the descendants of those who drove Abraham out of Ur in the first place, now identified and demonized as the Muslims of Islam.

Like the suicide martyrs of other times, Jesus is reported to have been a man who sacrificed his life for a better tomorrow for all of mankind. I do not think he was trying to be a Muslim or a Jew or a Christian, or to make any such distinction. I think he was trying to say that we are all the children of one God and we should take care of each other. Sadly, we have gone to great lengths taking care of each other, but not the way he hoped for. Instead we have used his name and his beliefs, and instead of forgiving we chop off the heads, put them on sticks as trophies and parade them through the towns and villages, and all in the name of Christ, or Mohammed, or Moses, or Abraham. Hebrew religious leaders felt their stature was threatened by this heretical holy Man and his message of peace, for whatever reason they felt threatened and they nailed him to the cross. Even then he was forgiving and merciful to his murderers.

Jewish people have been persecuted since then. Wrongfully accused, it reminds me of a Communist slogan, one for all and all for one. It means all are guilty or all are innocent. A few people were guilty of the crime that has profoundly affected the human race.

I am not a student of the Bible, but I do seem to recall that the possession of the Promised Land by the followers of Abraham was contingent upon driving out the devils that were living there at the time. Taking such a story as literal might not be unlikely to motivate someone even today to consider a certain ethnic cleansing of the region to be God's intention. Even if a Palestinian Muslim would sincerely like to be part of Israeli society, what could he do in the face of knowing his Jewish neighbors deep in their hearts believe he is one of those devils God commands them to drive out of the Holy Land?

I do not know whether it is harder in these times to be a Muslim or a Jew. Like the warring cousins of what was Yugoslavia, the Arabs and Hebrews are cousins, both Semitic people. Likewise the contesting religions at heart share the same root in the ancient tale of Abraham, and how mankind came to be, and God's demands of mankind and His promise to the heirs of Abraham. The Holy War is a family feud, among factions of a common faith.

IT'S NOT ALL IN THE
MIDDLE EAST

A few years have passed by since the Lockerbie tragedy over Scotland, the bombings in Lebanon, the occupation and invasion of Lebanon by Israeli forces, and finally pulling the troops out of Lebanon. On both sides of every conflict have been groups of extremists, each supported by some pretty extreme governments. Ironically, Christian militia groups are supported by Israel. Hezbollah is supported by the Arabs and Iranians. Where will all this end? The Christian militia founder Bashir Gemayel, President of Lebanon, whose father and his militia supported Hitler during WWII. Now they are allies of the Jewish state. How can such people believe their acts are making some kind of overall or historical sense? It sure doesn't make any sense to me.

Arab states surely are not matched with Israel in superiority in the battlefield. As they cannot defeat the Israeli military, since 1962 they have taken a profoundly immoral position towards the Israeli people as well as their own. Because of the misrepresentation by the leaders of the Arab people, many radical groups have been born but do not blame their own leadership for their internal problems but blame the West instead. The radicals have all recruited unemployed youngsters with the potential for a bright future and no chance for one who had nowhere to go and nothing to do. Some received an education from the radicals and became destructive and dangerous and turned into murderers and some of them became very highly Western educated and trained professionals in different fields and became unfortunately like those who conducted the terrible attack in New York. It seems almost impossible that such despicable actions could be taken by people who were once innocent little boys and girls. They have been turned into monsters without mercy or compassion.

At the same time I have seen the Israeli government not trying to heal the wounds or trying to restrain their selves from doing the same thing as the terrorists are doing. They become terrorists themselves on many occasions, performing such dark missions as personal assassinations, supporting such groups as Christian militia in Lebanon, to the massacre of women and children in Sabra and

Shatilia. I thought being strong meant that you could be more forgiving. Instead I have seen the Israeli government in particular such men as General Sharon behave in ways that are very unwise, as well as being cruel and without compassion and mercy. His connection to the Falanchis is an immature or desperate move to counter Hezbollah and Palestinian guerrillas. Governments and people around the world were enraged that the Israeli forces stood on the sidelines watching the Falanchis killing Palestinian women and children.

Palestinians sometimes look like victims, and the Israelis like villains. Then in the next day's news, the Israelis' children are bleeding in the streets, and the jeering and cheering Palestinian radicals appear to be fiendish homicidal fanatics, slaughtering the innocent. In this case I think they are both behaving like bad guys. The energy they have spent fighting and killing, and money they are receiving from around the world should be put to good use building homes for all of their people. There should not be armed national borders and the barb wires and concrete barriers, but instead parks, newly planted forests, building of new farms, communities, integrated by all groups, races and religions. Instead they have forgotten to do all of the good, and have perfected all the evil that we would wish not to happen to us as individuals.

There is an ancient story about a selfish man. When a house was on fire in his neighborhood, he heard about it, he saw it, but he didn't do anything about it. He said the house was not near his own so he did not worry about it. Unfortunately, things didn't happen the way he expected. Strong winds started blowing, and they blew the fire from his neighbor's house toward his home, and his house caught fire. Though he had not helped them, he cried out to his neighbors to help him. "If you had helped us when the fire was started, your house would not have caught fire," they reminded him. Then they participated in helping him to put out the fire. He learned the lesson of being part of a community. Many countries in the world seem not to have learned that no matter how hard we try to ignore our neighbor, we are still involved in some way in each other's life. When the great forces of the world like fire and flood and famine come upon us, we are all neighbors, and none of us can expect to stand apart from the others caring only for ourselves. If we do not stop it together, the fire will sweep through all of our homes. When I read about the suffering and the horror going on in countries all around the world, I find myself linked to every corner of the globe and to all the people around the globe.

During the war in Yugoslavia, I experienced the loss of many loved ones close to my heart. I watched on the television screen, on the major networks, live performance of the terrorist army of Yugoslavia, now Serbia, shelling the city of

Sarajevo from the tops of the hills, firing thousands of shells, indiscriminately killing women and children who are their own citizens. One of those citizens was my very first grade teacher, Ruzdija. What a horror it is to remember that I was once a member of that Army of Yugoslavia, and what a tragedy it is that unlike my American veteran friends, I cannot stand up and look back with pride upon my military service. I vowed to myself then as I stood watching the Bosnian hell on TV, that I would never stand on the sideline again and be a spectator to any war. I will raise my voice in a peaceable way, hoping I can find a way that I can touch or change the hearts and minds of anyone who has thought to pick up arms to harm another human. Although I know that my voice may or may not be significant, I know that there are many people just as I was, who can be made to see clearly the dangerous course that our world has embarked on, and who will do what they can to help put out the fires.

During the war in Sarajevo, the Israeli government chose to support the Serbian government of President Milosevich. Today they are all being tried for crimes against humanity for killing two hundred fifty thousand people while trying to impose Serb dominance over all the people of the former Yugoslavia. The Israeli government clearly knew the government they were supporting was wrong, and they still chose to do so because of the political differences of the Middle East. Ironic as it may seem that mortal enemies, Iraq, Syria, Libya, and Israel were all in the same boat on that matter, each supporting the massacre of Bosnia and Herzogovina. I would have expected, because of what happened to the Jewish people in Europe, that Israel would be on the front line to defend the weak who are being persecuted for their ethnicity and their religion. Sadly, it did not happen. There is a famous saying that those who do not learn from history are doomed to repeat it. Of what use is history to people who will not even learn from their own experience?

From Libya, Syria, and Iraq, I would have expected cries for the protection of the Bosnians as Muslims. Yet for various reasons of political or international significance, the Islamic nations of the Middle East turned their backs on Bosnia. I suppose I should not have expected more, as their behavior in the last forty years towards their neighbor, Israel, has shown time again that they do not truly have in their hearts the moral values their ancestors once treasured, the moral foundations of family and good neighbors. This is a great tragedy, and a great blasphemy in the lands where Prophet Mohammed announced the message of peace from God. I have never claimed to know or understand everything about my religion and Koran. One thing I have been most moved by in my knowledge of it is that Islam is compassionate, merciful, and forgiving. Islam teaches us to be clean, strong, and healthy in body and soul. Islam teaches everything I could hope to know about love of life, love of family, love of God, and love of all that God has given to us on this planet and in the universe. I don't think one can ask for more than that.

Political conflict between the Arabs and the Israelis has showed certain things about them. As Hebrews and Arabs are both Semitic people, they share many of the characteristics of people who have evolved in such a hard environment. They are both passionate about their tribal loyalties, and they are not likely to be indifferent or even lukewarm toward others. They love you or they hate you, and there is no in between. For them to hate each other is the same as hating themselves. If the Prophet Mohammed and Jesus returned together and told them they were brothers, the love for each other they would have upon reconciliation would be a passionate and unbreakable bond. If they fight, they are both doomed to hell on earth. I myself would not wish to have to stand against either the Arabs or the Hebrews, as both of these Semitic people have proved themselves through the centuries to be very formidable.

Are we humans destined to destroy ourselves? Will we be destroyed by the advanced weapons of our minds because we failed in the simplest matters of the heart? Do you remember as a child seeing the reflection of your face in the water? To me, that was always like magic. I cannot recall the first time I saw myself in a mirror, but it has always been fantastic to me to see the reflection of myself there like magic, and to think that someone thousands of years ago made such a small technological advance. A little mirror had replaced the reflection of water and shadows on the wall and the one who possessed the mirror had thus risen one step above nature. It is such small steps above nature that have enabled us to survive all that the natural world has thrown against us.

Throughout history that ability to take such steps has delivered us through the wind, the fire, and the floods, the rise of oceans, through earthquakes and volcanoes, the droughts and the ice ages. It has enabled us to rise above the crocodile and the tiger, and to rise above the tapeworm and the bacillus. All that nature has thrown at us we have survived, although we should not forget we are part of the body of that nature that has insured our survival. Today, we are at a crossroads of disaster, as each of the powerful people and all of the powerful movements in the world seem to be completely irresponsible, prepared to destroy all of the world in order to be personally remembered in history one way or the other. Do they not realize there will be no one left to read the history of their damnation through their pride and self-righteousness?

Have you ever gone to bed and thought of not waking up to see another day? Not because of heart failure, or getting hit by a car, or clubbed with a baseball bat by a robber, but instead because of some lunatic who is holding his finger on one of the thousands of nuclear warheads that we have created to defend ourselves from each other? Just who are all these people who take their religions and their politics so seriously, who believe God wants them to kill people who wear hats in church, or who do not? These are people who think in all of mankind's history nothing is more important than their flag, or their king, or the name of their little principality. Some of them think there is nothing more important to the destiny of mankind than getting themselves elected or otherwise put into power in some country or other.

There are dozens, perhaps hundreds of people all over the world holding the triggers to atom bombs, from the constantly drunk lunatic former president, Boris Yeltsin, of the former Soviet Union, to the ambitious and egotistic French, the ever proud English, the paranoid Israelis, or the hungry and poor Pakistanis and India's Hindus who had nothing to lose, to whatever bureaucratic nightmare is happening in the Army of China. Such powerful people tend to be obsessed with their own job descriptions, and they take their uniforms as more accurate self-identity than their skins. Having roles high in power in the great pyramids of social structure, they tend to see those structures as being more important than the people who make them up, and therefore able to easily justify killing any number of people to protect the integrity of their church or state. In fear of each other, many of the world's powerful governments have created their own dooms-day weapons just as good as everyone else's.

Then there are a few abused children around the neighborhood as well, and they are waiting for the chance to take advantage of even a moment of payback time. Wouldn't you look for payback if you were a little kid in the neighborhood being pushed, beat up, kicked, abused by whichever of the big kids happened to live closest to you? These are our human brothers, Israelis, Pakistanis, the ancient people of Ukraine, the Afghanis, the Kurds, and the oppressed people of a dozen countries in Africa. All of these people feel a great lack of ease about the rest of the world. They have been given no reason to think that anyone in the world is going to stand up for them when they are getting screwed. For sure they are ready for payback time. They have no nuclear weapons, but they have just as good a baseball bat in their hands as everybody else, and even if they come from very small places, they still are human beings who care about their lives and their families and their rights. They have been kicked around forever, so if anyone is looking again to send them to Hell, they should know that they are the ones who already know where the road to Hell is. Rest assured if you try to take them on that road, they will show the way there with no charge, because they are angry and restless. They may be charming enough not to show it as they shake our hands going down the street to the diplomatic meetings, but I warn you not to make them mad. I would hate to become better at prophecy than Nostradamus.

There, in the heart of Europe, war had broken out in Yugoslavia once again. I had tried for many years to do something about it. I had written letters to the leaders around the world, the most mighty and powerful. I plead for the life of my forefathers' land to be spared, from the massacre that happened in the mid ninety's to the beginning of 2001. I had little success saving the thousands of innocent women and children, but I have learned one important lesson. I must always try to show my neighbor that I am a man and human just as he or she, with compassion toward all life and love and family and neighbors. We are reflections of one another. People in Bosnia were the same as all of us. They have contributed to the world through the centuries a mosaic of themselves in a cultural and intellectual way, which somehow has been overshadowed by people who thought they were better or deserved more.

During the Serbian crusade through Bosnia, the world stood on the sidelines and watched the show on their television sets in the luxury of their homes. Can you imagine what King Dario of Persia, Alexander of Macedonia, the great Saladin of Syria, and the eras in time such as the Hellenistic Dynasty in 330 BC what such people would have thought if they had television like I do to watch their destruction of each other? In this greatest time civilization has ever known, when we are capable of traveling great distances almost instantly with massive armies, which after all are created to protect the weak from oppressors. History has taught us nothing, nothing at all. In the beginning of the twenty first century, in the best times for mankind, hope for drifting away from oppression and a bully neighbor, the Western world and Europe in particular, which I am part of, we have just allowed and given clear passage to President Milosevic and his Serbian and Montenegro army to pillage and plunder a land of Bosnia and Croatia. We as Westerners stood on the sideline and watched all of that happen. How could that happen? Are we just pretending that we are civilized men, or are we barbarians who are capable of hiding in sheepskin but instead being real wolves, predators who have no mercy or regard for the weak, and waiting for the moon to rise so we can howl at it without feeling guilty or remorseful that we haven't done anything wrong? We didn't kill the sheep, someone else did. In that case it is a man who is on trial now in The Hague for crimes against humanity, Milosevic. Looks like since they caught the guilty man it's almost vindication to the West, who has shown no remorse.

My parents taught me that one should forgive but not forget. I certainly shall never forget what I have seen, and I confess I do not yet have the spiritual depth to forgive those who have done such terrible things, nor to forgive those who stood by and let it happen, nor to forgive myself for having been so complacent in my beautiful American dream that I was able to do so little. God forgive me, I could not stop them.

STILL A BOSNIAN, AMERICAN?

I was at my home in Las Vegas enjoying a rare day off. I had just recently had a child born, the first one I was able to and chose to be there with, and I watched the miracle happen right in front of my eyes even though in my Balkan culture men should not be participating in the birth of the newborn. How beautiful nature has created and balanced all the things that we little humans take for granted, and are not yet capable of understanding. I lived in a beautiful home in one of the most spectacular cities in the world, and my family was safe and healthy. I could afford to feel separated, insulated from the rest of the world, above the trials of the world like a man living in the clouds, like Dario, the King of Persia, or the Greek gods of Olympus. If Dario and Apollo had telephones, what would they do in a time when they might at any minute receive a message as I did?

It was almost ten o'clock in the morning I received a call from my friend John Coletta, from Caesars Palace. Our friend Reno Armeni was talking in a loud voice behind him, saying, "You had better come out for lunch like we had arranged. I haven't seen you for a long time, and I miss you. I don't like missing you, I want to see you."

"Reno you are just like your great father, God rest his soul," I replied, knowing they were on a speakerphone. "You just love to try to intimidate your friends, don't you? I'll tell you what, if you have any of those cigars that your respectful father and Winston Churchill used to smoke together, then I will come just as you say, on the double."

"Angie, you are great at giving compliments," he laughed, "and I will accept it from you because I know it is sincere, but unfortunately I don't think I can fill my father's shoes. I am only my father's son."

I said, "Reno, you are a successful man. Your father would be proud, and I am proud to have you as my friend. If your father could just see you as an executive at one of the best resorts on the planet, I think he would approve. Everything he would see in you is a man of integrity and character. I will not miss that lunch, I promise I will be there at ten o'clock sharp."

"Wait a minute," John said. "I have called to ask you a favor. Could you call your friend in Singapore at the Marriott Hotel, and put in a word for me? I have heard they have an opening for an executive chef over there."

"Why would you want to leave Caesars Palace?" I asked.

"I tried to convince him to stay, Angie, but he wants to go to Singapore," Reno said. "Maybe it's because you have always told him yourself how beautiful it is in Asia. I will ask no more questions."

"Consider it done," I replied. Unfortunately for me it was done, and my friend moved far away to Singapore.

By the time I got to Caesars Palace, Reno and John were waiting inside for me at the restaurant Primavera, with my espresso waiting for me and already very cold. The moment Reno saw me coming through the hallway he stood up raised his hand as he always does and said, "Better late than never, my dear brother, and I'm not signing the check. You are paying. I am always losing more money on your espressos than any other guest in the hotel."

I laughed, spread my arms, and we kissed each other on both checks. I said, "Don't panic, Reno, I will drink it even cold." Of course I couldn't pass John without kissing and hugging him too.

A host with a telephone met me, a man I had also known a long time. "Sir, Angelo, a man from Switzerland has been waiting for almost a half hour on the phone, will you take it at your table please?"

"Who is on the line?" I asked.

"He said he is your friend, Peter from Zurich, in Switzerland."

It was not good news. Peter had not been my friend for a long time, and I could not imagine why he might be calling me, much less why he would say he was my friend. Whatever it was, I did not expect that I was going to enjoy it.

My table was all the way in the corner overlooking Caesar's pool, probably one of the most beautiful pool areas you have ever seen. Even discomforted by the call, I was consciously aware of being impressed by the beauty and grandeur of the great casinos, their marble floors, luxurious carpets, gilded ceilings, and fine furniture. I have seen the ruins of the real palaces of the Caesars, and I do not believe they could have been more splendid.

I shook his hand and in my hand as always was a good tip that he knew to expect. The free breakfast always cost a lot more than if you had paid for it, but those who understand the spirit of Las Vegas know that tips are the life of the joint, and if you want that spirit to love you, you give tips like you were lighting candles on an altar. Maybe it is superstitious to think that a place or a thing can have a spirit, but I have always felt that if the spirit Sin City loved you, you could have anything you could imagine, and if it didn't, then everything you touched would suck a little of your blood. For myself, it has been a love affair from the beginning, and through the winning and losing streaks, she has always treated me most generously, maybe better than I have deserved.

The last time I saw Peter, I told that Croat kraut to his baboon-butt face if I ever saw him again, I would cut his balls off and pack them up his nose with the heel of my hand so far his brains would squirt out of his ears. He knows I can do it, too. He was a big red-haired strawberry-nosed craggy-faced guy with lean muscles and a hard attitude, a tough guy. Being an American patriot comes first for me, and close upon it my deep feelings for that cluster of quarreling states and cultures once called Yugoslavia, where he and I both have roots. We were pals once, compatriots, conspirators, and co-adventurers in international intrigue. When we made our moves, the lives of thousands hung in the balance, and the fate of our countries and our people as well. Those brought us together. In the end, I suppose it is fair to say those things also set us apart.

"Hello, Peter," I said. "What do you think you want?"

"Angie, I'm coming to pick you up," he said, just like nothing had happened, "and don't worry about tickets. I need to see you. This is not bullshit."

I laughed and said, "You're looking for a valet parking job?"

"I should be so lucky," he said. "I will be there in two days. I will take a cab from the airport to your house."

I had my mouth open to tell him to go screw himself, to go screw some other dog from the gutters of Zagreb like himself, but I knew I should hear him out. "All right, Pete," I said with a long patient sigh, "call me when you get to town." There it was, and he was back in my life again, like a dog you just can't get to go away.

Peter is a few years older than I am. He was one of Marshal Tito's bounty hunters during Tito's reign in Yugoslavia. These were secret soldiers who slipped in and out of many countries all over the world, investigating, intimidating, and sometimes assassinating people who had left Yugoslavia, but whom Tito still suspected of being dangerous to him.

There were hundreds, perhaps a thousand recruited just like Peter to ensure Tito's survival from his enemies outside and inside of the country, including a few who became notorious, such as the assassins Arkan and Shashalj. These dark men built their reputation as undercover agents overseas for Marshal Tito. Peter was one of their team members. Arkan is dead, having met his fate in his gambling establishment in Belgrade with a hundred rounds of bullets tearing into his body, a message from his best friend Slobo Milosevic.

Peter and I had become acquainted through some of the intelligence community people I had met trying to assist in the support of Bosnia. On one visit to Las Vegas from his home in Gold Coast, Australia, he noted that he had to go to Columbia for a business trip, then to Dallas, Texas, where he had contacts in both intelligence and in the underworld. He liked to brag about the things that he does. He asked me if I would like to go with him to San Diego to meet some of his friends from our intelligence service, but he didn't specify which branch that was, FBI, CIA, or Naval Intelligence. He sure knew how to get around. As well as working with several of those agencies, we both became involved in events that led to the breakup of Yugoslavia, and the creation of the independent Bosnia.

I enjoyed working with him. Though he was a crude man, usually smelled bad, and had questionable loyalties, I believed he really had the best interests of the Bosnians at heart. In his work, he was quite ruthless, but cool. I suppose it might have been because of his father's German blood that he was more detached and efficient than the passionate character of the Montenegrin like myself. Though I am long away from the valley of Gusinje, it is still my nature that I do not feel quite able to trust anyone who does not become impassioned about what he does. A heart without passion is like a hearth without fire, and I find it difficult to feel at home with either.

One of the finest people I ever got to work with was a mysterious long time veteran of the intelligence service, a man named Giles W. Pace. Perhaps he really deserved to be called the American James Bond, I don't know. In looking back, I am surprised at how little I knew about who Giles worked for, and what his job was. His background and his present life are both a mystery to me, but I always knew he was a true patriot, and a man who seemed to know the powerful everywhere he went. He and Peter were at dinner in my home one evening, discussing one of the many recent times the government of Yugoslavia had used the power of the army against the Bosnians. What I heard Peter say to Giles was like being struck in the face.

"The fucking Muslims deserve exactly what they got," he said. "They should have figured it out a hundred years ago, when their Empire fell. If Tito had run them all out, Yugoslavia would be a major European power today." There it was, the truth exposed that Croatian or not, he was still Tito's man, and no friend of the Muslim. He did not have the Bosnians' wellbeing in his heart, and clearly had to be motivated by some other factor. I could hardly guess what that might have been, but I knew then that Bosnia was just a job, and the Bosnians were just a client group for whom he had no respect or love. I was cut like he had reached across the table and stabbed me with the carving knife.

Right at the dining table in the presence of my friend Giles, I told him, "My tradition as you know does not allow me to kick your ass here in my own house, where you are my guest. I swear you know and I know, particularly where you and I come from, that the Ottoman invasion and introduction of Islam was the best thing that ever happened to the Balkans, and brought five hundred years of civilization. You defame my people, and you dishonor me personally."

Through my life I have always liked to do things for people. All my life if someone needed something I would walk a mile or longer to get it for them without question or gain. As for Peter, I had helped him and his family to settle legally in the United States. Yes, I felt completely betrayed. I swore to him on my mother's grave, on the blood of all my children, that if I ever saw him again, I would cut his balls off his bleeding corpse and put them right in his rotten mouth.

There I sat at my table overlooking the pool at Caesar's Palace, hearing his unmistakable rusty voice coming from his chest.

"You would only call if you needed something," I told him. "All right, what is it?"

"Angie, this time I don't need anything, but I have something you need very much," he said.

I laughed wryly, and said, "Peter, the only thing I need is another couple hours of sleep. I've been working very hard trying to stop the war in Bosnia, for your information. I just had a dinner event at the Polo Towers. There were more than eight hundred people, local and state politicians, and it was sponsored by my good friend Steven Cloobeck, who happens to be Jewish. I was so surprised to hear him speak to the audience, expressing his feelings on the war in Bosnia. I can tell you, Peter, I can't thank him enough. I will never forget the help that he gave to us. Our keynote speaker was Bosnian Ambassador Alkalaj, and our lieutenant governor was a guest of honor. What makes you think I need anything from you?"

"Listen man, that's all fine what you said," he said gruffly. "I'm glad those people are working with you, and you should call all of them right away with what I have to tell you. General Ratko Mladic is attacking Srebrenica and he is going to massacre the people."

I was stopped short. I couldn't even gasp, "What are you talking about?" I could hear the simple truth in his voice, and I knew he was not lying to me. I had of course been following the events in Srebrenica closely, and what he said was the fulfillment of my fears. Not even Milosevic, that shifty and treacherous little would-be fascist, would dare to turn the army against the very people it was supposed to protect, and to kill them because they were Bosnians Muslims. Yet he was clearly telling me that was exactly what was going to happen.

"I'm telling you, Angelo, so you don't say that no one tried to save the Bosnian people, at least from the Serbs' side," he said.

That caught me by surprise. "Wait a minute, Peter, what do you mean the Serbs' side? I thought you were German and Croatian."

"My mother is half Serb and half Croatian," he said. "I've been doing some work for Belgrade."

"Well that's great, now I know everything," I said. "You are truly a bastard. What else is new?"

"Just like I said, mister," Peter replied. "General Mladic is rounding up all the men and boys, almost eight thousand of them now, I think, and he's going to kill them all. There is nothing I can do from my position to stop it. You better do something if you can."

I was astonished that he had called me, as though he was only trying to make me feel helpless and guilty. "What would you like me to do, Peter, rub the magic lamp and ask for three wishes? If I were that lucky, I would not remember my childhood being hungry and poor. Eight thousand people is a catastrophe for any small country to lose. It's blatant genocide. Nobody would do that, not even the Serbs."

"Well, if you don't call somebody in Washington to tell them to intervene, I'm telling you eight thousand people will be dead, maybe ten."

"When?"

"It could start in hours, maybe a few more days."

"Peter, how do you know this? Who is giving you information?"

"You forgot Angelo? I'm the Jack of many trades, but none professional."

"Pete, you are not the Jack, you are the joker, always with two faces and both lying. That's why I never trusted you, but this time I think you may be telling the truth."

"General Yankovic is an old man, and it seems he feels some compassion," he said. "Remember the people that you met in Zurich from Badnja Luka, that guy whose brother was killed by Bosnian forces?"

"Sure, but I wouldn't trust that guy with anything," I said. "He's a Serb."

"Hey look, man, he got the call from the General, and I'm calling you, so don't give me any of that Serb shit," he said. "Now you better quit wasting time if we are going to save these people."

"What about this trip?" I asked him. "What's that about?"

"Just yanking your chain to get your attention," he chuckled. "If I was really coming, I wouldn't let you know about it until you saw me. Good luck, my old friend." He hung up.

"Okay, Pete," I said to the dead phone. "Okay. You can keep your balls." Apology accepted, but I don't forget the man can change colors like a lizard, and probably doesn't give a shit about any of them.

I got right on the phone and called the Bosnian embassy in Washington D.C. "This is Angelo in Las Vegas," I told the receptionist, a tight-voiced woman on the other end of the line, who identified herself as Jasmina. "I met the ambassador at a conference here, and he will remember me well. I have some information of international importance to him, and I'd like you to put me through to him, please."

"I'm sorry the ambassador is not in his office," she said, bored and flat, as though I had called to sell her Girl Scout Cookies.

"I have a very urgent message, a matter of life or death," I told her. "I know you are always able to reach him in an emergency, and this is an emergency. Will you please connect me with the ambassador, as it is very important that I speak with him."

"I'm sorry, I can't do that. You will have to call back another time."

"Wait, you don't understand," I said in frustration. "This is too important for you to make a personal decision to ignore it. Ambassador Alkalaj must hear this. If you will not get me the Ambassador, then you must get me your supervisor."

"I don't have to do anything," she said, "and the ambassador is not available."

Well, there it was, all the mentality of every bureaucratic regime in Yugoslavia, or anywhere else, for that matter. Just give a little person a big desk, and they turn into little tyrants. I wanted to tell her, "You make me remember why I am glad I left years ago." Instead, I took a breath, and said, "Ma'am, Jasmina, you don't have to do this for me. This is for eight thousand people in Srebrenica who are all going to be executed by tomorrow morning."

"Yes, and flying saucers will make California fall into the ocean," she said. "The Ambassador does not have time for cranks with pet theories." She hung up.

I turned my computer on and patiently waited for the screen to come on. It seemed to take forever, and every second that passed by, I felt as if I was hearing Peter's voice echoing in my head, "You better do something, mister. I did my part, and you better do something." My first encounter was a failure. I felt like I supposed a screenwriter must feel, having a story that is of great world significance, but without any big contacts. To whom do you tell your story, and how do you get through to them, and what do you say to them? My story, upon which hung the fate of thousands of people, had been effectively stopped by the first little petty bureaucrat it reached, like a screenplay rejected by a sophomore reader with a formula checklist making an extra fifty bucks by reading two a day. It was as though the old order had never left. Innocent people are dying in the streets, people with no clue to why there is a war going on all the time, and the same old class of bureaucrats is eating good and running the show from both sides of the alley.

I set about to compose an email, directed to the Ambassador, in the hope it was not Jasmina's job to read his online correspondence. "In Yugoslavia, the bureaucracy didn't have to answer to anyone, at least not to ordinary citizens," I wrote. "Here in America, our leaders are elected officials, and they feel responsible to answer to their citizens in their community. Everyone is held accountable for their deeds by everyone else. I have a critical message for you regarding the lives of several thousand Bosnians, of the greatest urgency. I have asked your staff in the embassy to relate the urgent message to you, but unfortunately it seems the message was refused by a secretary who introduced herself as Jasmina. I venture to say if the information I possess is genuine, then you will soon be seeking a new secretary."

It was not until early the next morning that I received a call from the Bosnian embassy, from a private secretary of the ambassador, named Esmir. He was very professional and very polite. Moments later a soft spoken voice on the other side of the line said, "Mr. Angelo, Ambassador Alkalaj here. What can I do for you, my friend?"

I told him what I had been told, and he was very concerned, and of course took me quite seriously. "We in America do not waste our time with anyone who is not worthy of our time," I told him. "You, Mr. Ambassador, and your government, better convince American presidents and American people that you are worthy to them to save your life." I reminded him that a few years back the United States declared if the Soviet Union would attack Yugoslavia we would go to nuclear war with them.

"Yes, but only because of strategic concerns," he reminded me.

I reminded him that strategy is not only about military affairs, but also a nation's reputation. "You must convince the President that the Bosnian people are worth saving, not only for themselves, but also in order to save the reputation of the American people."

He was grateful, and as he was a man of action and of honor, he did everything he could, but the tragedy was inevitable, and General Mladic ordered his troops to execute, to murder, to slaughter the eight thousand men and boys they held in captivity in Srebrenica. That is exactly what they did, and they no doubt raped all the women, and the children too. That is how it has been in Bosnia for a very long time.

AMBASSADOR ANGELO

The Srebrenica massacre was a horror I shall never fully recover from. It would have been a horror even if I had just read about it in the newspaper, but to have known about it in advance, and to have tried to stop it, and to have failed…that was especially depressing. I had possessed the knowledge that might have saved all those families, if I had just been able to get it to someone who was powerful enough, and in the right position to use that power. I felt very small and helpless, impotent in the face of the world's problems. I was surprised one day when I received a call from Ambassador Alkalaj, and he was asking me to do something for him.

"I have a little problem and maybe you can make a suggestion," he said.

"When I have a problem I go see a doctor," I said, "and I always keep a couple of aspirin in my pocket, so if I pop a couple of pills hopefully the problem will go away."

He laughed and said, "Yes, I realize you Americans all live on pills, literally as well as figuratively."

"Let's just say we don't like to live in pain, and we take whatever will get rid of the pain. Whether that is good medicine or just escapism is hard to say, isn't it? What is it that I might be able to do for you?"

"I have heard you have in friends in high places in Mexico," he said.

"I don't know much of anyone from New Mexico," I told him.

"No, no, not New Mexico, down south across the border. I have spoken to the Mexican ambassador here in Washington D.C. He is afraid even to talk to me. What have I tried to talk about with him? Don't you know that Mexico has not yet recognized us as a country?"

"Don't tell me that, I didn't know," I said in dismay. "The purest Roman Catholic country on the planet has not recognized Bosnia as a state? That's pretty tragic, my friend."

"I have spent countless hours in Washington and the UN, and I have played tennis with the Mexican ambassador in Washington, and I get nowhere. They cannot talk to me officially until someone back home in Mexico City gives them permission."

"I don't think you should play tennis with any of the ambassadors from Mexico," I told him. "Let them know you are not there to play country club games like a lobbyist from the enchilada industry. You are serious. You should invite them for dinner and explain to them the importance of Bosnia as a people and a state. You Ambassador Alkalaj should not accept the propaganda that is seen on television every day of some news media and you should make sure that these people understand that there is after all a country such as Bosnia and there are people living in it in of all faiths and religions, Roman Catholics, Jews and everybody else."

"The Mexican Ambassador does not understand what the Muslim war stands for and that there is a Muslim people living in Europe," he replied.

"Pretty tragic, but I'm not surprised. The Mexican government and their people are a hundred percent Catholic and the government is strictly a internal government who does not care what is going on outside the national borders of Mexico and I believe they like to keep their people in the dark. They are an oppressive government although supported by our government and our administration. A reason for our support for the last seventy years of their oppressed government in Mexico is because Mexico is the our biggest trading partner and the has the largest ethnic immigrant population which counts almost thirty five million. So maybe if you tell the Mexican Ambassador we are going to need piñatas and strawberry pickers, you may convince him to come to terms for some kind of diplomatic recognition for Bosnia. You must explain to them that Balkan and Mexican culture are pretty close to each other, both built on the family unit, on respect for person and property, on deep religious beliefs, and the honor of each individual person.

"Let them know that as a modern nation in the free world it is very important and a moral duty of Mexico to recognize Bosnia as a state. Failure to do so will tell us nothing else but that they have abandoned the beliefs of peace that Christ himself has preached. Mexico is still a country, which struggles to find for themselves democracy and justice for all their people. We both have much in common, in regards to persecution and injustice in our countries. Bosnia is no longer just a part of a socialist power regime, it is a sovereign state, and for Mexico to recognize Bosnia will bring Mexico into closer participation in the world community. You are the Ambassador, Sir, and they owe you a great deal more respect than a tennis game."

"Angelo, thank you very much," he said. "I will sure ask for such a meeting as soon as possible."

It occurred to me then that even though I was not a politician or a powerful man, in my position in Las Vegas I had come to know many very influential people. That position, like many things in Vegas, has always been difficult to define. I have worked in several of the finest casinos ever built, and the great executives, great entertainers, and great players have been my friends, and the "uncles" of my children. My private business and work, in which I have been fortunately successful, gave me invisibility and flexibility, as well as an opportunity to use the lethal combat skills I acquired as commando specialist to teach extreme martial arts to the bodyguards of celebrities who became my friends. I was the one who "took care of things" that needed to be taken care of. When the special VIP guest would come to town, the casino executive or some of my friends would ask me and my other friends to take care of some guests of theirs who may just have arrived to town and say, "Angelo, see to it Mr. Big Shot has everything that he needs, whatever that may be." That I did, whether that meant having a good time he will never forget, or getting a little physical and slapping him around a few times, making him realize that here only the good boys have a good time. By being a good boy, you are always a winner, and that was sometimes my job, at the old Aladdin in the early seventies, the old Stardust, and the El Rancho in the late seventies. It is a tribute to my good friend and mentor, Edward Torres, a pioneer of the gaming industry in Las Vegas.

Meeting him was an unusual and memorable experience I will never forget. I had just been hired in the hotel to work for him as one of the food and beverage executives. At six o'clock in the evening, he saw me walking through the casino to which I was not stranger. I was well known and liked in the hotel by his executives and employees. George Maxim, Tony Farbia, Mike Coolello, and the legendary Paul Herb from Philly, old and beautiful people. Mr. Torres asked Paul, "Who is the young boy?"

Paul replied "He is a good friend of all of us here and comes to the hotel to gamble all the time, his name is Angie and we just hired him today."

Torres replied, "He reminds me of myself when I was young, ask him to come and have dinner with us." It was my first night at work and it seemed like I could not stay out of or away from trouble, it follows me wherever I go. I try to lay low and be invisible and end up becoming even more visible. Paul, Mr. Torres and I were sitting at the Apache bar, which was located in the middle of the casino surrounded by tables and gaming and the poker room.

Paul said "Angie make sure you drink and eat what Mr. Torres eats and drinks."

I looked at him and I laughed and I replied, "Don't worry Paul, I've been there before."

So I went straight to the bar inside the working area that I had inspected an hour earlier and made sure that his bottle of soda water was inside the fridge along with a snifter glass so it would be nice and cold. I served Torres his drink and made Paul and myself one of the same. Seconds later, I noticed a gentleman kind of staggering walking towards us and talking loudly, "You bastard you!" At that moment I wasn't sure to whom he was talking, although it didn't take me too long to figure it out. He was right in the old man's face. "I can't believe some-one hasn't killed you yet, you have fired and hurt so many people through all these years, you fucking bastard!"

There was no reaction from my new boss and owner of the hotel, Torres. He practically had no reaction at all. He was as cold as a glacier in Alaska. I was still inside the bar and with amazement I knew the bastard who was yelling at Torres. I said "Richard, you son of a bitch, what do you think you're doing? You little bastard, how can you talk to him like that? He is an old man. All these years you have worked for him and ate good and pretended to be a big shot wearing a black tuxedo so that you can look like one of the mobster boys, you ungrateful little rat. How is it that Mr. Torres hasn't seen that you are nothing and nobody all these years?"

Well, he forgot about Torres and his quarrel that he had with him. He reached his hand over the bar with a closed fist and said, "I'm going to knock you out."

As I was in front of him with the bar between us which was almost five feet tall, and least three feet distance across from each other, it was an instantaneous reaction for me to grab his right hand with my left and pull him slightly towards me using his hands as my balance and being so flexible, with lightening speed I brought my foot up between Mr. Torres and Paul and I kicked Richard on his right temple. As fast and hard as I kicked him he was spinning three sixty circles straight to the floor. I leaned over the bar and jumped right across to make sure he didn't have any bigger ideas and see if he could stand up, which he did, very unsteadily. I told him "Richard if you are smart, don't make a wrong move, I will hurt you this time."

He is smart without doubt. He knew to pull back and not be burned. He told Torres in a crystal clear voice, "Mr. Torres, if you don't fire this son of a bitch, I will take you to court and sue you for everything you have."

The response that I heard from Mr. Torres the owner of the hotel, a legend in his time, a man that would never blink in the face of another man, never heard anything Richard said. He looked Paul straight in his eyes and told him loud and clear, "You see, you stupid son of a bitch, you didn't believe me that he reminds me of me when I was young. He is my boy."

For a second I laughed, I found his expression of feelings that he liked me strange and very unusual. I said, "I had hoped that was as a brother not as a son."

Before he had the chance to say anything, Richard Forrester, his former employee, who he had fed and clothed and bought cars for, and made look good, said "You better fire him or I'm taking you to court."

To my amazement, Torres turned slowly holding up his hand to me as if saying, hold on Angelo, I'll be with you in a second. He replied to Richard "You are drunk and you are nothing and nobody and I'm sorry I was your mentor all these years. You are disrespectful and you are a disgrace. Now get out of here, and I suggest you get yourself a good lawyer."

I thought for a second he should be walked out with his feet forward. In the meantime the chief security of the hotel, Pete the Greek, was there to help him to his way out. That was the turning point of my relationship with my new boss. It was a fine impression on the very first day. I offered to quit so as not to cause a legal problem with the hotel. He responded by asking Paul which comp number for executives was available, comps A, B, or C. I was granted a comp as a special privilege, only for executives, which included a guest and unlimited room, food and beverage.

A month later I had the whole soccer team from the city of Zadar, birthplace of Constantine, now a part of Croatia, as a guest of the hotel. They were on a tour of the United States, more than forty people. They ate and drank for three days. Nobody spent a dime. Even the director of the bank from the city of Zadar was with them. I wonder if and how many of them raised their arms or weapons to either help or hurt the hopeless people during the war in Bosnia, and I wonder if they remember their friend, Angelo who treated them with a Roman feast at the El Rancho in Vegas, thanks to Edward Torres, my friend. Even in his old age he could be intimidating to someone who didn't know him. One morning I received a call at home from his room in the hotel and I was surprised it was Ed Torres on the line. Strongly voicing and demanding as usual he ordered, "Come to the hotel right away, I've got to get out of this room."

I said, "What happened, you lost your slippers, you can't find them?"

"No, I didn't lose my slippers! I was hurting all night from the operation I had, remember?"

"You mean to tell me you missed Hogan's Heroes and Sergeant Schultz last night?" I asked.

He said, "Don't make me laugh, it hurts too much."

"All right, all right, I'll meet you in the front of the coffee shop in about twenty minutes."

So we did meet and he greeted me with his cold expression as usual and by now very familiar to me and asked me, "How do I look? Do I look weak or sick?"

Honestly I replied, "You look good man." I gently put my arm under his and told him "Good to see you, you look well."

He gently stepped back, and freed himself from my arm holding his and looked straight into my eyes and said in his usual way with curses, "Look at these fucking guys here. I don't trust any one of them. They all tell me what they think I want to hear, like you look good, you look good. I don't feel too good myself right now. Toni told me already, you got canned from your job, and she loved it, she hoped you aren't coming back."

"Well if she said that, then can I have my old job back, or would you like me to be your assistant?"

"Don't be a wise guy, Angelo! Your lucky I'm giving you your job back."

"Hey did I call you or you call me, and I didn't ask for any job back." I said.

"Okay, okay you can have your job back."

"Look papa, I don't need the job, I don't really want the job." I said. "The only thing I like is hanging around with you."

Torres said, "no wonder Toni said you're a lousy worker."

So there we went in the coffee shop and had a lunch together as usual, and I ate exactly what he ate and drank exactly what he drank. Certainly his reputation and his road to where he got to was not without bumps and barriers, so one had to be careful having a conversation with him about who knew of whom and what they were, such as being a childhood friend of Mayor Lansky of Miami. There was a time when he owned the Rivera Hotel in the early sixties, as the story has been told, he had a boy working as a pot washer in the kitchen named Pavis. The next day he was promoted as a food and beverage director in one of the finest hotels. I wonder what he did? It was prestigious position with no doubt. As if the story is true or not I never tried to find out. When you are in a circle with the boys, quality people as they are, with honor and the strength of morality the code of conduct, the smartest thing to do is never to go in the grave yard and try to dig the corpses out and try to see who they are. Even if you know who the corpses are it makes no difference.

I have tried always to make sure I have never asked for anything material from anyone even from my friend, Torres, although I always know and I am smart enough to understand that if you are in the right circle you will always know that someone from that circle will need something that you have, especially if you liked adventures as I did. Sometimes I like to push people around or show off, but I have never abused any of my opportunity by being a bad boy even though I could and get away with it. I walked a thin line so that everybody saw that if it was time to be tough I had the strength and will to do it. So I was never was bothered by anybody from my circle of my people and everyone knew because I would show them in play the skill of my Kung Fu, to show them who the boss is.

I knew that made me a good man to know if you came to Las Vegas, but it only then began to dawn on me that I also had the opportunity to know and meet many celebrities who were very active politically off stage, and who might be able to do things that politicians could not. Even in the circle of gambling one would think that none of these people would be able to find their own city on a map of the United States, but you would be surprised, these people know many people and politicians in very influential high places. It occurred to me that all the adventures and good times and many times I thought of as time wasted, after all of those years, even the people from the southern border of Mexico that I have met, they became for me in some ways a hope of moral importance to give dignity and recognition as human beings from the Christian country to my ancestors, people across the ocean where blood has never stopped running. I would call it a forsaken place on the European continent and perhaps forgotten by God, and then again, there is a light of hope.

People like my friends David Garcia and Tido Peodrin were my lights of hope, as well as my good friend Carlos Santana, who all have influence in Mexico. Just as I had promised to Ambassador Alkalaj, I arranged a meeting in no time with our friend, Senator Amador Rodriguez Lozano. He was the speaker of the house of the federal government in Mexico. I believe he is right next to the president by title. With a few phone calls the meeting was arranged in Santa Monica, California and the next followed at the beautiful Del Mar resort looking over the sea of Cortez and Baja California with a breath taking view of the Coronado Islands. I was promised results not just a meeting. The meetings were successful and the recognition of the diplomatic relation between Bosnia and Mexico was moving forward thanks to my friends.

Then just when I was starting to feel proud of myself, for the moment my thoughts just went wild. I thought of Rwanda, of the disputed lands of the Israelis and Palestinians, of Northern Ireland, and many other places from which if people open their hearts a single voice can be heard as thousands die in torment. It made me feel a terrible rush of sadness and guilt and loss that I had not tried to do the same thing for the Rwanda victims, when a half million people were slaughtered by their neighbors. I promised myself that I would never be silent again. I will always try to bring attention if I have see injustice being done, and never fear that I can do nothing just because I am only one small person. Each of us is in the end only one small person, and it is exactly all of as individuals who can do such things towards the good of all of us.

I got my wish for diplomatic relations, and I had my meeting at Del Mar. I was asked by Senator Lozano when we were alone at the table, "Listen Angelo, are you sure you are not the ambassador?"

I smiled and reached across the table and he did the same, we held each other's hand and looked straight into each other's eyes. "I'm not looking for a title of any kind," I said, "although I will take a compliment from you because you are a man of influence and pride. Whatever you decide to do today, it will be a mark in history of your success in diplomacy in the twenty first century and you will give a chance to people you have never met, across the ocean in my ancestors' land."

"If I am able to do that, Angelo, I will give it to you," he said.

"Senator, dear sir, please don't bring your country more isolation. Use your good respectable office to bring about peace, a peace long awaited, for the Bosnian people. Your country has a moral duty to do it. I'm not begging for it, I'm asking you to do the right thing."

"That's why I want to give it to you, Angelo," he said, "because you are asking and not demanding, and it is clear that you are right. Here is my telephone in Mexico City and if there is anything urgent that you need, you make sure that you call me."

We had lunch and then he smiled and asked, "Where is the camera? This a historical moment."

I laughed. "Not so fast, Mr. Senator. This is just the beginning of historical moments for us. I know you'd like to take another picture with a famous guy like me. I was hoping you might remember the last time at the LULAC convention at the Hilton in Albuquerque, New Mexico. You and I and Jose Velez, the national president, and your friend Henry Cisneros, were all sitting around the podium, trying to reelect our favorites As you might recall, I got my title as Sergeant of Arms. I was so honored to be one of the few non-Hispanics to hold such a title. I hope you voted for me."

"I didn't, actually," he said with a laugh, "but I'll try to make that up to you."

Our next meeting a month later was arranged by Carlos Santana, and they brought with them as a member of their delegation a gentleman named Felipe Pavlovich. His ancestors are from Montenegro, and he has the distinction to be married to Tito's sister. I enjoyed his company, and developed a close relationship which has grown to this day.

Bosnian Ambassador Alkalaj and I tried and eventually succeeded in getting a promise from the delegation of Mexico that they would act for diplomatic recognition for Bosnia, as soon as their election was over. In early October 2000, I received a call from a friend in Mexico informing me that their party was losing the presidential election, and all we thought we had gained had been set back to the starting point. A new player will be in town, he informed me. "His name is Vicente Fox Quezada, and for sure he will be President of Mexico. Maybe it would be a good idea if you wrote him a letter before he gets in office. So he may look at it during his campaign, because as you know Mexico is very isolated in foreign affairs."

Again I had the inside information to give me a little edge on time, so immediately I wrote a letter to the man who would become President Fox. As I had to the Senator, I stated the importance of the events in Bosnia to world issues, and called for him to use the power of his new office to seek immediate action for righteousness sake. Some time went by, and Sr. Fox was elected President of Mexico. I was delighted to find out that the very first task of his new UN ambassador was to meet the Bosnian UN ambassador and discuss the terms of the relations of the two states. I was told by my friends that President Fox had jokingly said, "I don't need to receive another letter from Angelo, your friend from the States. The letter I've received from him well justifies our taking immediate action to see a diplomatic relation between our two countries."

Of course, Mexico did officially recognize Bosnia, and I felt I could take some sense of accomplishment in it. Was it because I felt more Bosnian than American that I became so involved in international affairs? No, it was because taking action to bring about a closer bond between two countries, two cultures, the one from which I came, and another I have only recently met, is a very American thing to do.

A PEACE CONFERENCE

One of my early involvements in the affairs of my country with respect to Bosnia was in September 1995. Kevin Donnellan, a hardheaded Irishman and world peace activist, succeeded in convincing me to try to organize an international peace conference for Bosnia. I wanted to know why he was doing it before I agreed.

"Angelo, I am not a religious man, but I have been in a war. As a Vietnam veteran, I have had my share of spilling the blood, mine and my enemies," he said. "I just think this is righteous."

Though I had known him a few years, we were not close enough to ask him personal things about his life, but I did. "Have you enjoyed spilling the blood of your enemies? Did you get enraged when you saw your friends falling next to you, and you just killed anybody you could?"

"You've got that wrong, Angelo," he said. "I didn't enjoy killing people, even when my friends were killed. Neither did I enjoy people trying to shoot and kill me. Vietnam was a bad idea and a nightmare that I myself and many other soldiers would like to forget about. This is not about another Vietnam, however, or any of that shit. It is about people in Bosnia who need help now."

For all his heroic action in Vietnam he was a gentle giant, who I swear to you looked just Santa Claus three hundred and sixty five days a year. The gentle giant was highly decorated in three tours in Vietnam, putting his butt on the line every day to protect me, to give my family and the rest of my country a chance to live in the peace and tranquility that I had dreamed of as a boy. I thanked him for his thoughts and his understanding about my ancestors' land. "You know, I find nothing more rewarding personally than to meet people like you, and to know about you, and the fifty thousand fallen soldiers who gave up their lives for me to be free," I told him. "There is nothing I can say to change the pain you say you would like to forget about, but I hope you believe me when I say I am proud of you, every one of you. Thank you for honoring me as your citizen."

To tell the truth, I think he found that a little embarrassing, as though he found it easier to be heckled than applauded. What a fine person. Of course, I immediately put myself one hundred percent behind creating a world summit conference for Peace in Bosnia, to be held in glamorous Las Vegas.

I went to see a friend of mine at the Riviera, Jimmy Paxton, a hotel executive. As he had always been courteous and sincere with his friendship to me, I wasted no time asking him if there was anything he could do to organize and facilitate a space and rooms for an international conference to bring peace to Bosnia. He wasted no time in responding, "When would you like to have that done?"

I replied that I wanted to schedule it in December, and I had a list of people from seventy countries to be invited from around the globe.

"Hold for a second, Angelo," he said, and he dialed a number. "The guy coming down to meet you is Robert Vanucci, the president of hotel operations. He is a great guy and he will take care of everything."

"Wow," I thought, "Jimmy, I am grateful for your friendship." That is one of the things I love best about Las Vegas. It runs on heart, and if people care for you, they will put the big powers in motion for you. My thought drifted back to when we had first arrived in town from different backgrounds, and when we met the first time at the old El Rancho Casino. I was there every day with my friend George Maxim, president of the hotel, and with the owner Ed Torres. He had always called me son and always asked me if I needed anything. I always told him his friendship is enough and always gave him a hug and a kiss on both cheeks and received the same exact back.

"If you need anything, you know where to come for it," he said. I laughed at that expression, but Jimmy always said not to, because he was serious about what he said.

"He really loves you man, you really remind him of himself, the way you do things and the way you carry yourself as a tough guy," he told me.

Now there you go again," I said to him. "I'm not a tough a guy, I just am a proud man and I have high principles in everything I do, and I treat my friends with respect and will accept nothing less. So remember, Jimmy, I want your respect because I deserve it, not because you think you have to give it to me. I love you as a friend and I respect you and I know if I ever did need anything you would always be there just as you are now."

He reached over the corner of the dice table we were leaning on and wrapped his arm around my shoulders. In the middle of the casino where people were rolling dice and playing and screaming, their emotions all wrapped up in the game, probably seeing nothing else but the dice table, covered with red, green, and black chips, we forgot all of the commotion for a moment and we had genuinely embraced each other in bear hugs. Almost in the same instant we separated from the bear hug and looked each other in the eyes, and just burst out in loud laughter, almost crazily.

"We have come a long way, haven't we baby?" he said.

"Yes, we sure as hell have, and I tell you it has been a beautiful journey," I replied.

About that time Bob Vanucci showed up and said, "Hey you guys, quit making out in the middle of my casino."

Jimmy laughed again and said, "Angie I'd like to introduce you to the president of our hotel."

Bob declared any friend of Jimmy's is a friend of his, and we shook hands and embraced as if we had known each other all of our life. I told him briefly what I wanted to do with the conference. There was no hesitation from him to facilitate the place to hold the conference.

"These are not ordinary people, Bob, they will be ministers, ambassadors, Kings, Queens, and Presidents from more than seventy countries around the world."

He whistled, whewwww and said, "That will require some heavy security. We'll need to involve Metro, but I will call Sheriff Moran, so that should be no problem at all. We should also coordinate with the FBI."

"Well, I guess you have to do that with the FBI," I said, "but my pictures are in their files already. I think I'm probably pretty famous with them."

"Don't worry about that," he said. "I will make a few calls and let you know what I can do as soon as a do a little research. I'll need to call some of the other hotels to facilitate some rooms, because all of these people will need suites, and special rooms."

"Those rooms will cost a lot of money, Bob," I pointed out.

"Don't you worry about that, all these people love to take pictures with the big shots," he said with a chuckle.

"What people?" I asked innocently.

"The owners of the hotels," he chuckled. "You know, they are all just like star struck kids too, when the celebs come around. They trip over each other trying to get them to stay at their places."

About six o'clock that night, I had a cocktail with Jimmy, and he told me Bob had been impressed and enthusiastic about the project. On September eighteenth, I sent letters around the world to a list of such outstanding and influential people as President Clinton, John Major, Harry Silajazic of Bosnia, Chancellor Kohl of Germany, Jacques Chirac of France, the late Senator Patrick Moynihan, whom I greatly admired, and Prime Minister Yitzhak Rabin of Israel. (How tragic it is to look back on how he lost his life in cold-blooded murder by a deranged fanatic, gunned down in the public square of Tel-Aviv by one of his own citizens. A great loss for humanity. The dream of peace for his people has been shattered since his death. He was a great leader and it was a great loss.) I sent the invitations and received in a matter of days a letter from a respected office of President Chirac, addressed to Kevin Donnellan as representative of our organization.

"We are always excited to hear opinions from a people like you," the letter said. "We are concerned about the war in Bosnia. The conference that you have suggested to be held in Las Vegas is strategically too far from the area where the troubles are. If a conference needs to be held it should be somewhere else, perhaps in Washington, D.C."

A few weeks later, I learned with amazement and I admit some dismay that he had organized the same conference as mine. He held the conference in Paris exactly as I had stated in the letter, including the agenda of discussion and the purpose of the conference, some of it word for word regarding the war and bringing a just peace long awaited for the people in Bosnia. My conference plans were of course made redundant and superfluous. Even so, I could hardly complain, as insofar as Chirac might have been motivated by my efforts, at least I succeeded in one way toward bringing influential people together to try to stop the Milosevic machine'of war from wiping out Bosnia.

I have seen the French government, at least through my eyes as an American, being dishonest toward the war. I have only seen them give genuine support to the Serbian aggression against the people of Bosnia. Unfortunately, with sadness, I have seen that most of the western world at the beginning of the war and some Arab middle eastern countries like Syria, Libya, Iraq, and Israel have done the same, supporting the war machine of President Michalovich of Serbia, and of Slobodan Milosevic.

The effort to organize the conference had set me in motion, and I found I could not just leave it alone and go back to my regular life. I thought I should take initiative to write as many letters as I could to every senator of ours, and I did. I tried in a most profound way to explain and try to bring the picture into their faces of the crying and dying children from the horror of that war. I explained to them that Bosnia could be a very important ally to us. I asked them what could happen if we do not take actions to stop the slaughter, not in Auschwitz, but in Bosnia. We should step in and intervene immediately to prevent genocide of the Bosnian people, I told them. I have written to many senators and representatives, and have met some of them personally. I have studied each senator with the concerns on their agendas and their responsibility in the Senate so as to better present my point of view to them related to their point of view. In that way I wrote the letters so that they would know that I have individually addressed issues of their own past history, to the present conflicts and possible visions for the future. In some way I succeeded at least to bring it to their attention.

I have a hard time accepting even now that the world stood by in the sidelines, almost like being in a Roman arena or a soccer field watching a game. This was not a game. Thirty thousand children have been slaughtered in the course of that war, and two hundred thousand men and women disappeared from the face of the earth. Today in the history books of Bosnia you will not be able to read anything about this.

AGENT ANGELO

With associates like Peter, and friends like Giles Page, it should have been no surprise to me that I met and worked with several agents of the American intelligence community. It was a pleasant surprise, all in all, as some of my previous experience with the agents of the world had been quite brutal. But the men and women of the American undercover services I met have every one been people I can look back upon with fondness and respect. It was not, as I had seen in oppressed countries, an experience of being coerced and used, but instead one of being permitted to assist in a worthwhile cause. I told myself it was not just the James Bond romanticism about it that excited me, it was something very real, and very sincere. I have had many contacts with such people over the years.

During the war I was asked if I could lend some military knowledge or advice that I might have about the former Yugoslavian military. I replied without hesitation, with utmost sincerity, "Our boys are in harms way. Our Air Force and Navy and Marines are all today fighting the communist army of Yugoslavia, today's Serbia. You do not know how capable they are or what kind of fight they will put up. I will do it, and I will give you my expertise and my knowledge the best way I know how. I will strive to be fully credible and truthful, so that if ever you applied the information that I have given to you, it will benefit our soldiers, and prevent harm from coming to them. If I can do that, I would be happy to sit down and talk with you. I have instantly realized that I have a once in a lifetime opportunity to really give something back to my country that has given me everything I've ever dreamed of."

As recently as July 2002, had the pleasure of receiving a call from Long Beach and San Diego California from a lady I had long known as an agent requesting a meeting with me. I asked if they would like to meet at my home in Las Vegas but they declined. Instead she replied, "I have reserved suite at one of your favorite places, on the Howard Hughes Plaza." She is one of those people I wrote about whom I wish I could applaud by name, but who has to remain a cryptic Agent G1. At Howard Hughes plaza where the meeting took place, on the ninth floor of the hotel, I spent more than six hours exchanging conversation and thoughts about the war, about the people, about the politics, and many other things, on military strategy and the readiness of the Yugoslavian army. They wanted to know if I was prejudiced against anybody or anything in any way. I stated there is absolutely no place in my heart for any bias about anyone or anything because I myself have been prejudiced against by others.

The meetings had gone very well. Agent G1 and her partner Agent G2 questions at times were very aggressive, straightforward and personal but I found myself feeling very comfortable and each question that was thrown at me I answered without hesitation and even at times laughing. I know that I had one chance and only one. Not to convince them of any lies but to make them believe and understand that I am a true patriot and ready to give my life. I know giving my life or dying for my country or for any cause is not the thing to do, it's being smart and living and finishing the things I'm supposed to do, because if I am dead it accomplishes nothing for myself and my country. I have found myself in a group of professionals and diehard Americans, men and women, who I have realized that their service has given me a chance to enjoy all the beautiful things that I had never had before I came here to America. Now it is my chance and I have been given an opportunity to serve my country, not just as a guy from whom they were needing a little information but as one of them, a fellow American, to serve and keep our country free and free from harm from anyone. I find myself feeling tall, proud, honored, and most fortunate to be one of few to make a difference.

When they asked me how I felt about the chance of the Serbs leaving Kosovo, I said, "What are you thinking? I have given to you before specific numbers of the paratroopers and special police forces, about seventy thousand of them, but all you have told me that those are unrealistic numbers and how do I know that? These people are volunteers from Montenegro and Serbia and hard core extremists. They are on the payroll of President Slobo Milosevic, including the current Governor of Kosovo, Sheshelj, and the notorious rapist and murderer, Arkan. They are nothing more than a bunch of thugs, murderers and rapists. There is absolutely no way we should let these people, these murderers, leave Kosovo alive. They have burned and looted and killed from the borders of Austria and Sylvania, through Croatia, Bosnia, and Herzegovina to the banks of the Drina River. Now they want to win the battle of Kosovo and as we are speaking they are putting people on trains on a one trip to hell just like Hitler did during World War II. I am not here as a Kosovar or as a Yugoslav. I am here with you as a fellow American and soldier that you have honored me for a moment to share my knowledge because our men and women of our armed forces are in harms way. Those Serbian thugs will not hesitate one second if they get an opportunity to harm our forces. We should show them from our strength, morals and military point of view that there is no way in hell they are leaving Kosovo without paying the price of their lives for the damage they have done."

Agent G2 asked, "What do you suggest Angelo, how do we stop them? That is rugged terrain, there is no way of stopping them."

"Don't you worry about that," I replied. "I know every single rock of those mountains and hills and roads. I rode the wild ponies bare back through the rocky hills of Cakor just as the Native Americans did here in the West. I know every single road and there is only one way out and one way in. At the of Mountain of Cakor, east of my home town, above the city of Pec, there is a high straight wall of a mountain, with deep gorges, almost a mile, and there is a road carved right through the middle of the mountain, which connects Montenegro and Kosovo. We will blast it with our air forces, that road, and blow up the bridge in Murina over the river Lim. There is no way they can even try to come this way."

Agent G2 asked, "What will their reaction be to where they will go?"

"They have to go back to hell or Pistina," I said, "because there is a strong Serbian underground base. From there I think they can go to Krusevac and I hope when they reach that they will all drown in the South Morava river, because that is a long way to Belgrade from there."

We said farewell after all of the meeting and agreed to meet again very soon. The bridge at the river Lim was blown up hardly without a fight. It was a success with no loss of our lives or the civilians of Montenegro. That was a proud moment for me as a citizen of this nation and being able to participate for a better tomorrow and the freedom of mankind, which after all my country stands for, freedom, liberty and justice for all. Just as I have said many times, you have to be alive to make a difference and be patient. Agent G1 and G2 and I had developed a personal bond and understanding with mutual trust and respect for each other.

G1 and I had made it clear to them that I was not after any kind of a James Bond adventure. "I will consider this with the utmost importance because our soldiers lives are at stake," I said. "Anything that I do or suggest that could affect the safety of our troops I consider carefully." I insisted that they should have some more contacts from Yugoslavia who are knowledgeable in military and intelligence matters about Yugoslavia, so as to better apply my suggestions for any military actions. I'm proud to say that all of my suggestions, political, psychological, or military have borne fruit. Each time I was informed about the success of the previous suggestions that I had made.

They have always tried to thank me for what I'm doing. I have always found that offensive, and I have told them if you try to use that word again, I will not meet with you again. "I am first an American. The only thing that connects me across the Atlantic Ocean is my ancestor's. Whatever we are doing here together is my duty as a citizen of this great nation of ours. To make sure, that our men and women fulfill their duties and keep in check our strategic, political, and economical importance around the world. I hope you get that crystal clear from me. Please quit making me feel as if I don't belong here, as if I was an outsider."

"Oh no, please, that's not what we were thinking at all," Agent G1 assured me. "Washington is grateful and they consider very seriously every suggestion that you have made. I am grateful about that bridge on the river Lim that you blew up yesterday. I heard the whole valley was shaken up from the explosion."

Agent G2 laughed out loud, "It was a spectacular mission, and it was just as you said, very hard to fly low, because of the high slopes of the two mountains and that high horn peak at the middle of the valley, a very narrow entrance. The pilots said they felt as if they were flying through tunnels. The mission was successful just as you suggested and hoped for."

I told them I take my position very seriously, as I know that when I am speaking of military knowledge, any mistakes I might make would have consequences beyond my comprehension. I couldn't bear the thought of making a mistake, and then seeing coffins coming here because of my error. I am proud to say that everything that I did saved lives on both sides of the alley, or at least I've tried.

I once suggested we should move our fleet aircraft carriers farther back in the Adriatic beyond twenty five miles off the shores. I remembered that when I was still in the Yugoslavian Army, I had taken a small part in the creation of a fleet of tiny torpedo boats intended to defend the coast from ships of war. Yugoslavian defense had made torpedoes and Russian made scuds that were a danger to our fleet. How many of the floating robots still existed, I had no idea, but I knew in the hands of the wrong people, they could harm our fleet. I was hoping that they would hear me, but of course that is not the kind of decision I might hear back about. My suggestion was well taken and we did move our fleet twenty-five miles inside the Adriatic Ocean and we have flown thousands of missions over Yugoslavia with only one loss of our stealth aircraft over the Belgrade area. I had suggested in many of our meetings, that we should blast the chiefs of staff headquarters inside of old Belgrade, instead we made a mistake for some reason and went and bombed the Chinese Embassy, of course not too much of a big error. I thought that was a great mistake, China needed to get a bloody nose for supporting Serbia.

I called my friend in San Diego and in Long Beach and as they say in California, I was "stoked" with excitement even though it was a mistake. Still I was hoping that we would go and blow up the general headquarters of the military in Topcider and in the heart of old Belgrade, just behind the hotel, Slavia. All the generals are in the building at six o'clock in the morning. I told them, if we chop off all the snake's heads there will be no snakes to bite. In my disappointment, we blew up many buildings and bridges around Belgrade, even the Presidential Palace, but we didn't blow up the building that I really wanted to blow up. I told my friends, almost a hundred years ago, on the river Lim where we blew up the bridge, there was a war where the general, or as they called him in those days Vojvoda Marko Miljanov, left his soldiers drowning in the river in the late fall and got saved by hanging on to a horses tail swimming across the river, him and seven other men. How great or unfortunate that history has to repeat itself, they lost again and this time by the great American military force who fight only to protect the innocent from the oppressor.

Agent G1 and Agent G2 requested that we should get together. I said, "I can't wait my friends, and are you buying dinner? Boy, I wanted to have that prime rib from Circus-Circus steak house. After all this success we deserve a good dinner, and the government is paying for everything, right? No life was lost in Montengro, in my hometown, isn't that great?"

G2 laughed and said, "Hey what are you trying to do, read my mind even before I said anything? I am buying and I'll meet you tonight at six o'clock at the steak house."

We said goodbye, and I called Circus-Circus hotel and asked the operator to connect to the Steak House. On the other line I heard the voice as always gentle and professional, of my friend Ron, the maitre'd. Angelo, my friend, long time no hear from you! When are you coming to see me? I miss you, you bum."

"I love you too, Ron," I said. "I shall be there tonight at six with two of my friends and my wife and children."

"I haven't seen the children in a long time, and I miss them," he said. "I want to see them. Please make sure they come along. Have they grown up?"

"Well let's say every time I look at them, at how they are growing so fast, I turn to myself in the mirror and I see every day I am older and wiser man and good husband, father and friend. How is your family? Is everybody all right? Do you need anything?"

Ron replied, "I love and respect you and you are always my best friend and all I need is your friendship." I've been blessed since I came into this great land. I thought having friends like Ron with such a diverse ethnic background and yet we had found understanding, respect, love of life and family, and love of the country that we live in and a common ground of the highest respect that one can think of. Not as with my friend Peter, the man who slept in my house, ate my food, and drank my wine and yet wished nothing good to come for me, in fact wished me dead. Fortunately, people like Peter have made me stronger and more determined to not lose at anything I put my mind to, no matter how hard or how easy. G1 and G2 agents arrived and we had dinner at the steak house. As I predicted it, the check was already taken care of, not by our government or taxpayers' money, or not by me, but by my respected friend Ron.

My wife declined to go eat with us, and instead took the children to the indoor amusement park to give me and my friends space to talk about our next agenda concerning military actions in former Yugoslavia. We sat at the far corner of the room until late in the evening drinking only coffee and sodas, and compared notes and our progress of our armed forces which at the same moment we were speaking they are at a harms way in former Yugoslavia. I must admit, it seems satisfying and gratifying to look back at our success, the lives we saved and kept millions of people from harms way. We agreed to meet again soon regarding the air force of Yugoslavia.

I had a meeting on one day specifically about the Yugoslavian Air Force and ground to air defense. I had warned my friends that we should be careful the way we fly, how low and how fast. We may lose some planes if we are not careful. They will not use the radars because they know we can knock that out. They will use the radio and the telephone to let the guys know fifty miles away that the plane is coming at a certain speed and height, and that is where they will get us. It is very primitive, but effective. The next day, Scott O' Brady was shot down, apparently without having been observed by active radar, which his airplane's electronic surveillance equipment would have detected.

We sat for many hours, six or seven hours in our hotel suite, going over the military maps from Yugoslavia, marking with yellow and black erasable inks, places from Belgrade to Nish and Podgorica and many other places through Serbia. How can we stop the movements of the army, an army that had no control? There is the governor of the Province of Kosovo, who controlled seventy thousand so called militia, blood thirsty loyalists of President Milosevic and his henchman Governor Sheshelj, the same notorious blood thirsty killer who worked for Tito as an undercover agent through the United States, in Chicago, New York, Los Angeles, and Cleveland. He was even decorated and ordained by the late King Alexander's organization in Chicago with the title of general. Sheshelj undoubtedly has the blood on his hands of many migrated workers of Yugoslavia throughout the western world, no doubt with the help of his friends, like Peter and Arkan.

I offered Agent G1 a gift. "The biggest fish you are looking for," I said. "What fish?"

"Remember the last time we met at McDonalds at Hughes Plaza, we talked about the man named Sheshelj?" I asked. "Peter has spoken to him on the phone from my house, and introduced him to me over the phone. Sheshelj trusts Peter with his life, so I can deliver him to you on a plate. If you want, Peter and I will just make him disappear, or if you want him as you stated at the last meeting of ours, I'm ready to hand him to you at any time, without a single hair missing from his head."

She sat back for a moment with a look of surprise in her eyes, as though surprised that I was telling the truth and not joking with her. I could clearly see also a fear of danger, and of being dismayed that I thought that was what she and her agency would likely want. "Angelo, we cannot do that," she said patiently. "We are not in the kidnapping business."

"What kidnapping business, who's is it talking about kidnapping anyone?" I asked. "The man is a notorious murderer, with blood on his hands up to his heart. I have not personally seen him kill anyone, but he is commanding the deaths of thousands right now through the militias. I have no idea how many people he is responsible for killing when he was Tito's agent. You want him, I can get him for you."

She replied, "No, absolutely not. We are not kidnappers, and we are not hit men either. Can't you imagine what that could do to this country's reputation?" I thought about Nicaragua, El Salvador, and Guatemala, Peru, Honduras, Chile, and Argentina from 1970 to 1984.

"Well," I said, "there are many people like Peter and Sheshelj, and I do not think it is wrong to recognize them for what they are, and just go out and get them. I once went after one of those thugs myself, a guy named Alija Delimustafic. Does that name ring a bell?"

"Oh, yes," she replied, "He is one of the biggest gun runners in Bosnia."

Agent G2 asked, "Angelo, what are you driving at?"

"I just want you to know and understand that I do not flinch from the idea that sometimes the best way to handle a situation is to dispose of some person or somebody who is doing no good," I told them. "There are some people I think it would be justice, and righteousness, and also smart to dispose of, and if I can help you dispose of them, I would be pleased."

I did not go into the details with them about my own previous attempt to dispose of Alija Delimustafic. Some time ago, when I was in Zurich, Peter and I were supposed to pay for and deliver some guns to the Bosnians. Peter introduced me to Alija, who was supposed to supply the guns to Bosnian forces in Mostar. Instead, he tried to get his own pet racket project going.

"You give me the money and I will build a highway from Bach to Budapest," he said. "It will do more good than arming the Bosnians to sacrifice themselves. I can put you on the payroll, as an international consultant." In other words, fuck the Bosnians, his interest was only on how to get control of the money, even if it meant building the Serb Express, and he had the nerve to try to offer me a payoff. I wanted to kill the motherfucker. That is not a metaphorical or hyperbolic statement. I meant to kill the motherfucker dead as dirt. I asked Peter to arrange a meeting with Alija that night, so we could go for a ride.

"Where are we going?" asked Peter.

"In the countryside, up in the hills," I said. "I want to teach this bastard a lesson so that no money in the world will help him. He doesn't know I'm from the old country also."

Peter looked in my face, and I think he understood that I was very serious about my intention. "Okay, Angie," he replied, "I agree he needs a lesson, since he is a punk who thinks he is a hot shot. Alija has some money with him and I think it should be taken from him. He wouldn't put it to good use anyhow, and we can kick his ass and let him go."

I could see he was back-pedaling, so I agreed easily. "Okay, you're right. Let's take his money, since it's so important to him, and scare the shit out of him. I think we need some tools from the hardware store. Is there a hardware store here?"

We walked arm in arm, Peter and I, right through old city of Zurich, down the hill, across the bridge, past the Chinese restaurant, next to the office where Peter had worked at times, meeting with world weapons dealers trading everything from land mines to triggers for nuclear weapons for Pakistan and many other third world countries who wanted to develop nuclear weapons. Peter bragged to me that the Russian General wanted to sell him some high-grade plutonium and some Yakovlev Yak 36 and Mig 23 fighters for two thousand five hundred dollars apiece, depending on the quality, from some countries around the Black Sea. I told him I had some doubt about that. You just don't carry plutonium in your brief case. It's kind of hard to transfer. I told Peter there is an American expression "hogwash" and I wondered if he knew what it meant. He kind of shrugged and didn't respond. So arm and arm we went.

The hardware store was not very impressive, two stories high, with a balcony second floor like some I had visited in the old mining ghost towns of Nevada, nothing like the Home Depot I had come to take for granted in the good old US of A. As we walked around the store, he didn't ask what we were looking for. I picked up a fine strong five-inch ice pick with a big wooden handle, a thin sharp shiny stainless steel spike. I saw the fear in Peter's eyes when he saw what I picked up. I looked at Peter and before I had a chance to say anything I saw everything in his eyes.

"Angie, I don't think he will show up," he said.

"That will be a big disappointment," I said. "I promise you I won't make a mess and you can take his money. The bastard deserves to die. He has helped Chetniks buy guns to kill my brothers and sisters, and now he wants to rip off the entire Bosnian people. And the son of a bitch is a Bosnian, himself, a fucking traitor."

"Angie, he told me last night he did not like the way your hands look," he said. "He asked me why your hands look so strong like that, and I told him you were a professional martial artist. I can tell you that he did not like what you said last night to him."

"What was that, Peter, that he did not like?"

"When you told him that Bosnia does not need friends like him," he said, "that the Bosnian people do not need enemies when they have friends like Alija. So I think he will not show up."

Lucky for him he did not. Looking back on it, I believe Peter probably knew right from the start that I intended to kill Alija, and he warned him himself. At the time I believed that Peter had warned him, in fact I'm so sure of it that I feel that it is of historical importance to show the negligence and ignorance of Alija Delimustafic. On record is a copy of a power of attorney which was issued to Peter on May 17, 1993 in Wien, Austria. Signed and stamped from the BH Bank of Bosnia, this document gives Peter power to negotiate business and to approve loans with the full power of the bank, of which Alija was president, stating in part, "That I Alija Delimustafic, Minister Bank President of BH Band of Sarajevo…do hereby appoint Mr. Peter Fxxx…as my lawful attorney in fact…exclusively to negociate business transactions in regards to promissory notes…as he may deem fit…as though I myself have so performed it…" It was as though he had simply given the entire bank to Peter.

Alija took treacherous and irresponsible actions with disregard for what his actions would do to our Bosnian people, and the consequences, which were with no doubt, grave. Did he know that Peter was no friend of our people, the Bosnian people? I am not sure. I am only telling the truth of what happened. If he had sold guns to the enemy or given them any financial help or cooperated to help with the enemy toward our people or any of those groups, he has committed a crime, at least in my view. No one has the right to play God, especially a little man such as him, with no experience in the political, military or diplomatic field. Whoever had given him authority to run the national Bank of BH and make him the owner of it, they must have known he was expecting material gains for his group of people that he was representing, or that he was supposed to protect the people of Bosnia. As much as I agreed protecting the Bosnian people from collaborators like Peter and Alija, who wanted to wipe out the Bosnian and Sandjak people from the planet earth, and harm the forces of the United States who are trying to protect the Bosnian people, I have equally cared to make sure that our young soldiers men and women come home safely. Last I heard, Alija is serving a long term sentence for crimes he committed against his people in Bosnia and Herzegovina and Sandjak.

At any rate, Agent G1 and her pleasant and efficient colleague Agent G2 made it clear to me that my willingness to swim with the sharks in the deep end of the pool was appreciated, but such activities were just not part of their way of doing things. So much for the Agent 007 stuff.

Agent G1 once requested for me to meet with a new contact, Agent G3 from the naval base in San Diego, California. We met in our usual place, or what had become my favorite place, on the Howard Hughes Plaza in Las Vegas just off the strip. Before I went to meet them I went upstairs to take my shower. Each step I was walking up, my mind was spinning a million times per second. What did the new agent want from me? What will he see in me? Somehow I didn't feel good about it. They told me he was a nice guy I should enjoy talking to, but there was something about the way it had been set up that set me off.

Each time I have met with any of our agents I have stressed to them that first I am an American and whatever I am doing, it is as an American. During my shower I started singing, which is unusual for me, an Italian opera, at which I think I'm very bad. I told myself, I hope you are a better convincer than singer, because today is the day I think will make it or break it. The new guy I think is thinking I'm too good a con artist, or I'm not telling everything I should be telling them.

I got out of the shower, dried my hair, splashed on Polo, my favorite cologne, put on my best suit, and I looked and smelled like a million bucks. I went downstairs and to the garage, started my 944 Porsche, drove to the Howard Hughes Plaza, and by the time I got to the lobby, one of my agent friends was waiting for me already. I had been asked before to speak to different agents, and I refused to do so. I was comfortable with the agents I was talking to and had developed a bond of trust with them. We have somehow a perfect reading of and understanding of each other and I didn't want to change that. If any new faces came in, I would have to readjust myself and repeat myself, and I do not like to do that. We shook hands and hugged when we met in the lobby as we always do when we see each other.

Agent G2 is well built, mentally and physically alert, always ready for any surprise, it seems like. You'd definitely like to have him on your side when you are facing the enemy. We walked toward the elevators, and during the few moments riding to the suite, he assured me that the agent I was to meet was really a nice guy.

"Don't worry, I just hope we will be able to communicate," I said. "Whatever he wants to ask, I will be happy to answer whatever I know, but I think I am running out of material. There is hardly anything that you and I have not talked about. We have gone through the military maps and plans, psychological military thinking, the warfare planning, we looked for everything, bridges, roads, factories, missiles, stockpiles, defense planning of the country, and defense of the Adriatic Coast, even the torpedoes. We have even talked about the chiefs of staff and the buildings in Belgrade, the military housing, the air force bases in Montenegro, Kosovo, and Serbia. I am not sure there is anything more we have not thought of."

The door to the room opened just as if they knew we were there, and I was greeted by my friend Agent G1. "Hello Angie, it's nice to see you," she said. "You smell delicious."

I laughed. "You know what the smell of Polo reminds me of? When I was a little kid we cut the grass and put it in huge piles, and if the grass was not stacked well, the rain and humidity and moisture makes the hay turn like a green mold and the smell is just like Polo. I don't really like it, but I wear it, because I don't know why but everyone else likes it." I wanted to hug her but did not. I thought I better be professional. She was in her mid forties and carried herself well, but I didn't want to make her uncomfortable.

They wasted no time introducing me to Agent G3. His handshake was limp and very weak, perfunctory. I knew in an instant that he was the kind of man who could be of a thousand faces and it would take me a lifetime to find one I could trust or feel comfortable with. I tried not to let that bother me, but after all we were not taking about sports games, but about matters of national security and life for our troops overseas. He didn't look impressive either. Pants not ironed, very dusty shoes, t-shirt rumpled, hair greasy, his face oily and sweaty, I did not find him neat or clean at all as I might expect from an ex-military man. With my experience of relations with people and the way that I live, hustling and trying to stay alive every day without being hurt or hurting anyone else, I have learned that you must keep your guard up all the time, and size up people before they size you up. If you are not better than them, you'll probably wind up six feet under, and not have time to regret meeting anyone. I was certainly never in any danger with my friends, but I for sure would not stand in the front lines beside Agent G3. He was a reptile, maybe a lizard, maybe a snake, but an emotional blank which would surely leave me cold. At least that's what I felt from him. I hoped I was wrong in seeing him in that way. Perhaps it was just part of his professional technique.

It was immediately clear he was part of a professional tactic. These people had become my friends, and they always respected my voluntary participation, but I caught on right away that this time they were supposed to put on the pressure, to see if they could make my story or knowledge of Yugoslav armed forces and intelligence crack. This time it was three against one, and they were supposed to take my story or knowledge apart if they could. Even being in friendly conversation, talking about football and baseball, if it's three against one you have no chance of winning. My conversation did not involve baseball. It was a very serious matter. They were sent by request from Washington D.C. "This time I better know what I'm talking about," I thought. "I should have a clear picture in my mind that anything that comes out of my mouth should be steady, convincingly loud, and clear. They should have no doubt of my truthfulness."

After long discussions, looking over the military maps, Agent G3 questioning me back and forth, trying to see if I'm twisting or changing or forgetting what I had already said, I thought of him, "Mister, I am a professor of psychology without the diploma hanging on my wall. If you are an enemy, God forbid, I think I could walk you across Lake Mead in Nevada and leave you thirsty on the other side without realizing that you walked on the water."

We shook hands and said goodbye. I did not say I looked forward to seeing him again, neither did he say the same thing. I was holding his hand in a strong grip without letting go and looking straight in his eyes, and said, "Mister, my ancestors' land is on fire, and you are here to find out what you can do to help put out the fire. Well, I may be a bad fireman, but I have tried and shot off my mouth for the last six hours, and I hope you don't think I talk that much all the time, because I usually charge when I talk. For this I just want you to know that I am a die-hard patriot of my country that has given me everything that I have dreamed of. Forgive me if you think I've talked too much. I just wanted to make sure that our American troops all come home safe to loved ones instead of in plastic bags. I doubt if you could ever understand how much I love this country."

There was no reply from him; his eyes were looking down to the floor. I let his hand go and said goodbye to my friends Agent G1 and Agent G2, and I rode down to the lobby. Agent G2 put his right arm around me and said, "Angie, I hope to see you soon. It was a great meeting. I sure hope it will save some of our boys' lives."

What an emotion I felt at that moment. I had finally heard what I wanted to hear from him, from somebody, all this time, the magic words, "our boys." He said, "our boys," and I felt deep in my heart, here I have a country of my own and I belong here. I am a part of the society of the most powerful nation on the planet. What a great time in history to be alive.

Sometimes people say that the Roman Empire and their citizens were so privileged. I can only say truly that if anyone has dreamed to be a Roman citizen, well, you don't have to dream about it. The greatest days of Rome were only a hint of what was to come here in America. If you are an American citizen and you live in this great nation, your dreams have already come true. Mine have come true, I can honestly say.

THE ISLAMIC BOMB

One night I came home, as usual I turned on the TV to watch the news and see what's going on in the world. I saw Senator Patrick Moynihan, always my favorite, a true patriot with a clear head and a true vision for our country. I saw him standing on the steps of Capitol Hill, and what he was speaking about astounded me. I wasn't sure I heard it right, but he repeated it several times. "The Islamic Bomb," he said. It brought chills to my body. I decided to write him a letter right away.

Dear Senator Moynihan,

I was very disturbed when I saw you on the television the other night speaking about India and Pakistan's nuclear arms race. You called Pakistan's an Islamic bomb. There cannot be such a thing. Was the Hiroshima bomb a Christian bomb because Truman and Roosevelt were baptized Christians? It demonizes Christianity, and insults the memory of Christ to say that weapons of mass slaughter can be an expression of Christianity. I am a Muslim like seven million of my fellow American citizens. We know that Islam is a religion of compassion, of brotherhood, of charity, and of pity for all human suffering. There is no way that an obscene bomb can be Islamic.

It is a good idea, however, that you call attention to this mindless rush to hell in south Asia. China did not destroy its missiles and bombs when and America and Russia did. I don't believe that China will stay out of India and Pakistan war which will affect its interest and its border. Can we then stay out of such a conflict? I suggest that you devote your talents to diverting the disaster out of approaching in South Asia. Defaming the religion of one of the parties involved does not help.

Sincerely yours,

Angelo Koljenovic.

I said to myself, here I am feeling good, telling myself I belong somewhere finally, and I see a man that I admire the most, standing right under the Abe Lincoln statue in DC and demonizing me as a citizen. I wonder for a moment where I can find a true home for myself and family?

Here is Senator Moynihan's reply.

Dear Mr. Kolenovic,

With the recent nuclear tests in India and Pakistan, we are closer to nuclear war than we have been at any time since the Cuban Missile Crisis. This is a challenge which requires the highest attention and the most subtle diplomacy and extensive discussions with India and Pakistan. Congress must also be involved in addressing the issues which arise from the nuclear tests in South Asia. The current sanctions regime provides no authority for the President to waive any of it provisions. The President needs the flexibility to negotiate in South Asia. And Congress should not adjourn before we have provided the President with the tools to reach agreements in South Asia. Most importantly, the President should go to India. The actions which we take to address this volatile situation will have profound repercussion on the future of the subcontinent and participation. We must talk with India and Pakistan as a matter not just of their survival but of our own as well.

Sincerely,

Daniel Patrick Moynihan.

It is a nice polite boilerplate piece that does not address the matter I wrote about. It is not an Islamic bomb. Are the bombs of Israel Jew Nukes? It is as though the underlying religious bigotry in his catchy phrase wasn't even noticed. The Islamic Bomb. It is such a horrifying idea that just to create such a phrase in order to make Americans feel threatened is in itself a form of terrorism directed against Muslims. Without even blowing anything up, it makes Americans see all of Islam as wild-eyed bearded fanatics, now with their hands on the triggers of atom bombs, each seeking the death of the infidel as the passport to Heaven.

Some time had passed and then Osama Bin Laden appeared on the front page of the news. He was living somewhere in Sudan. They said that he was connected with bombing in Saudi Arabia of our military barracks. Bin Laden was on the run. It seemed like everyone was looking for him. Sudan's government seemed like they were trying to get rid of him, but it looked like nobody wanted him. I thought, "Here is another bastard who is making Islam look very very bad and sending our religion with the help of Palestinians on a one way trip to Hell." He had left Sudan on his own to Afghanistan with all his of his millions of dollars. The US bombed Sudan, giving one more opportunity for the Arabs to cry we were persecuting them. In the meantime Bin Laden was settling down in Afghanistan, a country without law and order, buying everybody and anybody who could help establish himself as invincible leader of Afghanistan, killing and executing anyone who stood in his way.

A conference in Dayton, Ohio, for peace in Bosnia was a fresh breath of air to see coming from our President and our administration. I can only try to imagine trying to watch all the troubles around the world, and being responsible for having triggers to nuclear weapons, and having to come up with answers to everything. I wonder how every morning when the President goes in the briefing room, his head must be spinning on all the things that happened overnight. What is important and what is not? Sometimes I want to feel sorry for the President, but that is what comes with his job. He needs to lead and organize and safeguard our people and our country and the rest of the world. He also needs all the help he can get, so I wrote a letter to President Clinton and I suggested at least what the agenda should be at the Dayton conference.

Dear President Clinton,

My name is Bajram Angelo Kolenovich and I am an American citizen born in Bosnia. I'm certain that I don't need to tell you anything that is going on in Bosnia today. The terror and tragedy is in the headlines daily and daily gets more bloody. Myself and my associates have had some encouragement from American and foreign leaders. However, this process is slow and events are coming fast. President Slobodan Milosevic is undoubtedly coming under pressure from the extreme Serbian nationalists to whom he appealed to achieve his position, to intervene with the power of the Yugoslav army. The Croatian Serbs are losing and the Bosnian Serbs have been unable to force a decision on land. Their blundering is forcing the European powers to take tougher positions. There is a real danger of the entire Balkans exploding. It would be a mistake to think that the United States would not become involved. Two NATO allies, Greece and Turkey would be drawn in quickly and on opposite sides. Germany is heavily involved and France is pushing for greater involvement. The web of alliance and arrangements that served the United States so well since 1945 is too tightly woven. The United States will either become involved or damage those arrangements of living men. There Remember, there is not a border in this area that has not changed within the memory is no country without an ethnic minority nor a province that has not been fought over. I urge you to increase your efforts to bring the parties in the conflict to the bargaining table before events make the efforts futile. I urge you to bring relief to the Bosnians who have bravely defended their homes without adequate arms or powerful patrons. Whatever efforts you make now will be minor compared to the consequences of not making them. Your efforts now should be towards convincing President Milosevic to keep his army in barracks. Perhaps he can be convinced that military movement will not give him control of the situation, but will only decrease the chances of anyone gaining control. Keeping Yugoslavia out and bringing the Bosnians parties to the table is the only way to keep this wildfire from consuming the entire area and beyond.

Please do not think that because so many efforts are futile that new attempts should not be made. The United States wishes to be the world's leader because in part, no one else that might be can be trusted to do it. If you can lead this area to peace then the next challenge, no matter how complex, will be easier as a consequence. Failing here will make the next problem, no matter how straightforward, harder.

Sincerely,

B. Angelo Kolenovich

Here is the letter from President Clinton, whom I thank for trying.

Dear Byram,

I appreciate hearing your views regarding the situation in the former Yugoslavia. This past summer, I decided that the time had come to launch an all-out effort to achieve a peaceful solution to the conflict. I was convinced that the dramatic changes on areas in Bosnia, provided a window of opportunity to achieve a comprehensive settlement that could finally end the conflict. Since mid-August, an American negotiating team has been conducting virtually non-stop shuttle diplomacy with the parties to the conflict. Thanks to U.S, leadership, important results have been achieved. NATO air power has been instrumental in helping to end the siege of Sarajevo. In September, our negotiating team secured the agreement of the parties to basic principles of a peace settlement in Bosnia. These principles confirm that Bosnia will continue as a single, internationally recognized state within its present borders. Earlier this month, commencement of peace talks beginning on October 31 at Wright-Patterson Air Force Base in Ohio. Many difficult issues remain to be solved in the coming weeks, but I believe we may be closer than at any time in the past four years to a lasting peace in the former Yugoslavia. I have instructed my negotiators to spare no effort in clearing away the remaining obstacles to a settlement. Thank you for your interest in this critical issue.

Sincerely,

Bill Clinton.

The President stated he would like to clear the way of remaining obstacles to peace. The obstacles to peace were the people he was negotiating with. Today they are on trail for genocide.

I believe these letters are of historical importance. After receiving the president's letter I felt that his personal attention had been given to it. The conference that he arranged in Dayton was not a cure which any doctor would have prescribed. What I really mean to say is that any politician or leader if he would look back today on the conference, would call the agreement a failure. Bosnia today is still not a free society. It has been divided into three different so-called republics. I call one of them imprisonment, one containment, and the other a reservation. It reminds me almost of the white man coming to America and placing most native tribes in reservations so they wouldn't be a nuisance to the rest of society.

I am not looking to offend anyone. I am a European man myself, and I am not always proud of looking back at what my forefathers have done in history. There is much we need to apologize for and regrets for many things that happened. Bosnia is one of the latest sad chapters in history. The world has apparently quite purposefully given Serbia every possible opportunity to wipe out one group of people from the planet. Fortunately the people were resilient and have survived. The west had a change of heart, for whatever reason I will not ask. I am afraid I will get an answer that I already know.

Some individuals are paying for their deeds, but it's almost like looking at the stars. Does it make a difference to notice one that has just blown up? The trials are almost just as those stars in the sky. You might sometimes see the explosion of a few, but there is no change in the picture at all. It is just the same. The tragedy in Bosnia is a failure of human compassion. Why did my President hesitate to intervene, to save the lives of hundreds of thousands of innocent people? President George Bush Sr. wished not to involve himself in the conflict of Bosnia.

Butros Butros-Gali, secretary of the UN, has met with my President numerous times and his true colors have come out of the horse's mouth, as he himself called it. When the reporters asked him what he is going to do about all those children getting slaughtered in Sarajevo, he replied with no hesitation or compassion in his voice or in his face, "Well, Egyptians have been dying for the last thirty years, so what?"

Is it my fault because Butros-Gali's Egypt has not succeeded to win a single battle with Israel during their many conflicts? Well, don't blame me. I have one suggestion for him. Try to be more neighborly, more honest, and don't do anything to anyone that you wouldn't want done to you. My forefathers in Bosnia have been compassionate and merciful. What they have got in return are sharp swords with unmerciful thoughts, and the swords have made my people bleed beyond comprehension or repair.

I don't wish to blame anyone. I will quote some famous words from Mak. "Life is not that is mine for I am just one who stands in the shade of one who will fade with time." I wonder if he knew what was going to happen to his people? Did he cry when he wrote this? Did he greet his people in Heaven with the same words of hope as for the ones left behind?

THE CRUELEST BLOW

It was early in the morning, about six thirty, September eleventh. I had the late night shift, always a fast one in Las Vegas non-stop revelry. I came home and tiptoed around, as was my habit, to wash my face and my feet, change out of my work clothes, and put on my soft pajamas. I slipped in and kissed my two small children still sleeping in bed to tell them I love them, and then the same to my wife, who smiled and stretched to acknowledge her pleasure at my presence, but would like to doze another hour or so before rising. I went to my study room, turned on the television, and saw a silent picture that caught my attention as quite strange.

It was a still shot of the twin towers in New York with smoke through it, looking almost like a post card, or a station identifier. It struck it me as unusual for the local television news station to be showing pictures of the New York twin towers. An instant later the picture came back live. The smoke was real, and reporters were saying that a plane had hit one of the towers. At first it seemed less a horror than a curiosity. I was saddened, of course, but not stunned, and my mind was going through how stupid somebody must have been for a plane to hit the tower. The flames and smoke were getting bigger and bigger. I was listening to speculation from the reporters of what happened. They of course had no idea whatsoever, but that didn't keep them from blabbing away non-stop as usual as though they were the experts on everything.

The next second I saw the second plane hitting the other tower and I was instantly horrified and stunned. I knew in an instant that the world I had known was forever changed, and I was absolutely heart broken. Tears were in my eyes and I cursed and wept aloud, bringing my wife running from the bedroom. My hands went from my chin all the way up my face and through the back of my hair.

My first reaction was to call my brother and we both cried over the phone. I know we both felt the same for New York, and we felt a special personal attachment to the sad loss of the twin towers. We had watched the very last floors of the twin towers being completed in New York years ago, the perfect grand symbols of the wonderful country to which we had recently come.

The reporters were already saying it obviously was no accident. It was obvious that there was intentional harm. Whoever did it, they did it with the greatest and most resolute intention. When two more planes on that day crashed, one into the hills of Pennsylvania, the other into the Pentagon, there was no question they were sent to harm our country and our people.

I am sorry to say it, but right away I thought to myself, "Here they go again, it's the Palestinians." They and the Israelis are killing each other every single day as if tomorrow would be too late to die. Most of the time the Palestinians are throwing rocks and Israelis are throwing back with their sophisticated air power, American Apache helicopters and American F-16 fighters. From time to time even the bulldozers get into the action by leveling down the neighborhoods of Palestinian families. We have all seen Palestinian mobs in the thousands running in the streets in rage, challenging and screaming for revenge. So revenge it shall be every time. The cycle of violence has not stopped, because of the irresponsibility of the leadership of both sides, Israelis and Palestinians.

I have learned, I hope, to be cautious in judging or blaming or prosecuting anyone without real evidence. I am not a particularly religious person, though I am baptized as Muslim. I don't live by the strict law of Koran, I live by the laws of this land, written by our forefathers, as Abraham Lincoln said, "of the people, by the people and for the people." On the day of the bombing in Oklahoma of the Murray Federal building, I saw many people in the professional field of reporting express their feelings through their sophisticated wording of the English language, putting everything in the right perspective in their own way for their own audience, and they said just about everything except outright accusing Muslim terrorists of being behind it. I think some of them lost their jobs because of unjustified accusations. Every time I go to bed and I kiss my children goodnight, I am grateful for the officer who caught Timothy McVeigh. At least for once it wasn't a Muslim terrorist who tried to harm our country and divide our nation. I can truly say even though my heart was saddened with the tragedy that happened, I was relieved that he was not a Muslim. How unfortunate that I should take any satisfaction in such an idea. How unfortunate that in our great society, beautiful but not perfect, children can grow up with such hatred toward the leadership of a country that can give them everything they are capable of dreaming of.

My relief was short lived. Islamic extremists around the world are blaming America and the rest of the west for the sins of their fathers and forefathers. The hatred of the western world seems to have become almost uncontrollable towards any peaceable resolution. Here in America, if we don't like something we change it in the ballot booths instead of with bullets and bombs. They did not choose to do that. Instead, they took cruel advantage of the freedom of our miraculous air-line transportation industry, and made our beautiful airplanes into lethal weapons. They chose to hurt people who had nothing whatever to do with the quarrels they had in their own homeland. History has shown that our country is compassionate and caring, in spite of the terrible accusations people have made against America.

I have seen through the years we have a very fine tendency to forgive and forget very fast. Yet I think it will be a very long time before America ceases to blame all Muslims and all of Islam for the tragedy of that day. Is that a totally unjust accusation? Unfortunately, it is not entirely unjust. In my eyes there is nothing to be proud of in the historical fact that at least in my lifetime most of the leadership of the Islamic world has presented the Muslim as hateful towards anyone who is not a Muslim, and to see as enemies those who do not live by Islamic law. I resent that in the strongest terms. I think it comes largely from the mistake of using the mechanisms of the political state to enforce fundamentalist Islamic Puritanism. Islamic law, chosen voluntarily, might produce a very virtuous life but the enforcement of it by some elements in the leadership produces oppressive government and deadly persecution of all who do not obey. To attack America, or Israel, or any other country just because they do not live by Islamic law is a terrible crime, and a terrible tragedy, with cruel and long lasting results.

Like the pious Jewish fanatic who killed the foreign minister, Mr. Rabin, and the pious Christian anti-abortionists who kill doctors in the name of God, the Muslim martyrs who crashed the towers in the name of Allah have dealt to their own religion the cruelest blow. No one has suffered more from their insane and treacherous act than have we, as Muslims, all over the world.

I hope every Muslim in the world has a mirror in the hallway of his or her home. I hope that we all are able to look straight in the mirror and see the reflection of our own faces, as individuals, and how we portray ourselves and our faith. That we have forgot the dignity of the human life, I ask myself looking in the mirror, without fear, do you love life and respect yourself and others regardless of their beliefs? The reflection on my face was the truth, honest and genuine as I wish to see it in every human being. I am a human man and I love every one of you regardless of your beliefs and colors. I see no reason to be afraid to care or to be a good neighbor, a countryman and if I may say a citizen of planet earth. I find myself at times wondering what kind of future my children and the children of the world, have with such hateful people as the boys who flew the planes into the twin towers and into the hills of Pennsylvania and into the Pentagon in Washington D.C. killing innocent people. Even my own countrymen, sadly called the enemy of our people, Timothy McVeigh, the Columbine boys of the state of Colorado and others, I wish if I could tell them, they should travel around the world and see real injustice and then come back in our great state of the union and tell me what we are missing. The answer would be simple, we are not perfect, but we are sure the best since the Roman legion that hasn't been a democracy, in the country and the constitution that cares for their country as our great nation does.

As an old saying goes, if you have everything, you don't miss anything, and if you do not understand what you have, then it is very easy to lose it. If you never had anything, most of the time you never get the chance to know what you are missing. I have been given a chance myself, from having nothing to having the opportunity to earn everything. Am I about to give it up? No. I will fight for it and protect it with honor and dignity, against anyone who would bring harm to it.

A CALL TO
RIGHTEOUSNESS

As a man who is a father of three beautiful children, I love them all. My relationship to them differs, and they have different ethnic lines. How could it be possible that I could love only one and not all of them? The fact is that I do love them all is easily understood by fathers around the world. If our children are different, then we love them for their differences, not in spite of them, and our own hearts are made so much larger for that. Why is it so difficult for such fathers to see that God likewise loves all of us, without regard for our differences? We all believe the same truth, and that is that all human beings are children of one God regardless of our ethnic identity, our religious beliefs, or our national citizenship.

In the Bible it says somewhere that God is no respecter of persons. That means there are no earthly titles, nor powers, nor wealth that a man can possess that will make him something impressive in the eyes of God. I believe it is also equally true to say that God is no respecter of religious establishments, and no respecter of political powers either. The declared objective of all the religions and of all the states involved in this terrible tragedy is the same. That is to enable the faithful to live good, clean, virtuous, healthy, and prosperous lives.

We all believe there is only One God. The wise recognize that no description of God can be definitive, because God is greater than all of our human experience, and cannot be encompassed by any of our worldly metaphors. If any of us is right, therefore, it then becomes clear that all of us are right. There is One God, and we all hope only to be able to live peacefully and well in ways that will please God. We all claim to believe that, and we all claim to want that. Given today's miraculous technological control of our world, it is certainly possible. I will say a prayer for all of us under one God of many faces, one world of many cultures, one heavenly paradise of the greatest diversity and wonder for the world. Amen.

We stand together at the same destination, arguing about the maps that have led us there, each armed with nuclear weapons, and each prepared to destroy that paradise to make it uninhabitable to the others. What can save us from destroying and so damning ourselves at the gates to our earthly heaven? The answer is simple enough to say. It would be called a global epiphany. It would be nothing more complicated than for everyone to recognize and acknowledge exactly what I have just said. We are all seeking the same God, and we have all found Him. All we must do is to grant that each of God's children may choose freely to accept whatever religious form he wishes. We must each erase from our religions the terrible error that lies in the word ONLY and not make fools of ourselves as supposed civilized people who should know better.

"This is the only map, and this is the only way..."

"Only the seed of Abraham..."

"Only those saved by Jesus' blood..."

"Only the faithful in Islam..."

None of those is true, and believing them makes an idol of the God they describe, and creates bigotry among those who should love each other as brethren. *That is the truth that would set us free.* We have all fallen victim to the evangelists' frightening but effective little white lie, and we may then equally all forgive each other for it. I trust that when His children come to Him together in loving contrition, He will forgive us all as well.

Likewise we must have a political epiphany, and the answer is also very simple. It is described most precisely in the words of the Constitution of the United States of America, in particular in its Bill Of Rights. The governments of the world must recognize that their correct job is to protect the freedoms of their people, including the freedom to choose whatever religious form they wish in order to worship and follow God. Given such political freedom wise people will draw close to their neighbors and devote themselves to the common good. Given such religious freedom, pious people will draw close to those who share their faith, and celebrate the wonderful and bountiful world God has given to us.

Let us learn that the strict Islamic law, and also Judaic law, and the virtuous morality of Christianity are disciplines we are called upon to take unto ourselves voluntarily, as motivated by the Spirit of God. Our faith, as all agree, must be voluntary if it is to be accepted by God as sincere. The founders of the United States of America wisely included in the Constitution, and the scriptures of the Bible and Koran also proclaim, that such law must not be imposed by force, for then the people are motivated by fear instead of wisdom and righteousness. Worse, those who wield such force seem inevitably to become tarnished by it, and to self-righteously use it to impose a form of morality upon the unwilling, a sad hypocrisy. Let us learn that voluntary submission to the law our religions call upon us to follow does not compete with the necessary social order of secular law, but complements it, and gives it life and heart.

To live in voluntary submission to God in a place where the law of the land grants you limitless freedom is to enjoy the finest fruits of both political and spiritual enlightenment. That is exactly what the American way of life makes possible. It is the American way that the state, the constitution and law guarantees our freedoms, and it does not enforce nor suppress the practice or taboos of any religion. Each may live by the religious law he chooses, and none may use secular force to impose such law upon anyone else. The people uphold and protect the respected offices of the state readily and they follow and trust their leaders as protectors of peace and freedom. The people live by the tenets of their religions voluntarily, and through them they are moved by the Spirit of God to live peaceful and virtuous lives. There is no better or more righteous way.

Let us here in America, Muslim, Christian, and Jew, remember then to treasure that precious heritage, to protect it from being lost in quarreling over it among ourselves, and to keep our laws free and our hearts filled with compassion for all of our countrymen, and for all of our earthly brethren, under whatever name they choose for the One who is truly God. I don't want to quote from Koran or the Bible, but I wonder which one is the closet to heaven, a rich man or a poor man? Sometimes the poor man has only the goodness of his heart, the knowledge of his mind, and the sweat of his back, yet it may serve better than a gift of much gold from the rich man whose concern is for the appearances, the monetary value, and his social obligation. True, but how much more blessed is the rich man who is just and righteous, and generous with his wealth. I find my country very rich in materialism, the richest that has ever existed, but I also find it rich in their hearts and in giving to the needy all around the world. I remember when I was young, before I could read the words, I recognized the crossed handshake symbol with the American flag on every pack of butter or food goods that reached the four corners of the earth. I knew what that meant, even then, and everything I have learned since then about the great land called America that sent those joined hands all over the world confirms my belief that was an honest promise, many times fulfilled.

May God bless and protect this great land.

ABOUT THE AUTHORS

Bajram Angelo Koljenovic

Angelo was born and raised in the Montenegrin highland village of Gusinje. The grandson of an Ottoman officer, the son of a pioneer Communist, and one of the Muslim minority, he served in the Army of Yugoslavia before immigrating to the United States in 1969. He now lives in Las Vegas with his wife Man Kiu and their children, still doing the work he loves meeting people in the grand resort hotels and welcoming them from all over the world to his town.

James Nathan Post

James was raised near White Sands, New Mexico, son of a rocket radio engineer and an artist. He served as a helicopter gunship pilot with the 101st Airborne in Viet Nam, where he was highly decorated, including the Distinguished Flying Cross. He met Angelo living in Las Vegas, where he wrote a newspaper column and worked as a professional sports book player.

0-595-31282-9